Do Angels Smooch

Where do angels get the clothes they use?

PROFESSOR EDWARD KAPAMBWE

authorHOUSE

AuthorHouse™
1663 Liberty Drive
Bloomington, IN 47403
www.authorhouse.com
Phone: 833-262-8899

Published by AuthorHouse 05/22/2021

ISBN: 978-1-6655-2596-1 (sc)
ISBN: 978-1-6655-2595-4 (e)

Library of Congress Control Number: 2021909918

Print information available on the last page.

Any people depicted in stock imagery provided by Getty Images are models, and such images are being used for illustrative purposes only. Certain stock imagery © Getty Images.

Holy Bible, New International Version®, NIV® Copyright ©1973, 1978, 1984, 2011 by Biblica, Inc.® Used by permission. All rights reserved worldwide.

This book is printed on acid-free paper.

Contents

PART 2

PART 3

PART 4

PART 5

PART 6

Preface

People and angels; the unending saga. We are intertwined with angels like cotton and fabric. Western countries seem to be more fascinated with angels than any other cultures of the world with the exception of Israel. Something else has been brought to light, angels come dressed in human made clothing, shoes, jewelry and other necessary outfit that suit the occasion. Why do they use human stuff? They do that in order to infiltrate into our world, unnoticed. Many well-meaning song writers, actors and novelists, have bought into the idea that angels have wings. That is misleading. The other fallacy is that, people tend to convey angels as myths. Sometimes the angelic term is taken as metaphors especially in lyrics. For example, Charlie Pride who sang "Kiss an Angel Good Morning." To add icing to the cake, lo and beyond, the Trump campaign introduced another version of angels known as "Angel Moms". These and other angelic innuendos and phenomenon have compounded the need to dig deeper on the subject. To that end, it would be prudent to answer the following questions: Is angelic invocation a winning strategy in politics? Is that possible? Do angels come dressed in human attire? Where do they get clothes, shoes and jewelry they use? Why is hospitality the best opportunity to garner angelic visit? What happened to people who met angels in the past? Did meeting angels led to changed lives? Is it possible today to entertain a real angel? Can a real angel massage you? Trumpism and Angel Moms further compelled me to investigate the reality of angels. Did Angel Moms help Trump win the presidency? Are angels organized like human government? Something else dawned in my mind; no one has ever photographed a real angel; how then can we recognize them? If angels infiltrate our earth, are they able to smooch human beings? Is smooching a possibility? As they say, there are more questions than answers. This book has a lot of answers you least expected.

Introduction

What do Trumpism and Charlie Pride have in Common? Believe it or not, it's invocations of angels. Trump may have involved so called "Angel Moms" without knowing the implications of what he was doing. On the other hand Charlie Pride and others were merely using angels as metaphors in their lyrics. In any case, whether it's just a metaphor or inadvertently using Angel Moms as a campaign slogan, we know that angels affect human social settings in more ways than one. We do not even know how deep rooted they are in our communities. To that end, we will go deeper on our investigation of angels. If you followed the Trump campaign you will remember that at some point he introduced a group of women who called themselves Angel Moms. Besides that most of us know of course that the term angel has been attached to so many lyrics, books and now movies. What compelled and triggered me to add to the volume of books on our planet regarding angels were the lyrics and their emphasis on "kissing angels." But lo and behold they are now invoked in elections? Did some of you notice Trump kiss the foreheads of these Angel Moms when they disembarked from his podium? That is indeed was clear Trumpism! Why do lyrics emphasize kissing? Why the obsession about kissing angels? Then I recalled the book I have read many times. The good book also talked about angels marrying daughters of men because they were beautiful. These and other reasons require an in-depth investigation of angelic interaction with people. However, if indeed angels have been involved in human affairs from time immemorial to the present day, how do they participate in human affairs without being detected? How do they manage to get clothes, shoes, socks, shirts and so on without being caught? How did angelic mania begin in the USA? I mean who triggered angelic pursuit in US? Do angelic encounter bring good luck to people? Is there historical evidence that people who were visited by angels had their lives changed forever? Are there clues that we need to investigate to ascertain angelic visit? How do you know that a real angel visited you? Why does the good book emphasize the need to be hospitable as one of the criteria to have an angel visit you? What is so special in being hospitable to a stranger that compels an angel to visit a person? Perhaps one of the hardest questions to ponder is why angels come incognito? Why can't they just say I am an angel? That is what one of the angels said in the past; "I am Gabriel and I stand in the presence of God?" End of story! Zechariah then realized that he was talking to an angel. But if they come like strangers we will not be able to welcome and honor them?

Above all issues we shall discuss, what really intrigues me the most is the idea of smooching. Can angles still smooch humans to day? Did they smooch somebody in the past? The closest information to answer that question is found in Genesis chapter 6. So we will analyze that Scripture fully. For thousands of years, many have alluded to the existence of angels. Angels definitely do exist. But what is their role in human affairs? Better still, how do they help people if we do not even know how they look like when they appear among us? You will find clues in this book that can help you figure out if you were a host to an angel. How can one rely on someone they have never seen physically? Where do angels buy their clothes and what happens to these stuff once angels go back to heaven. All these questions are answered in this book.

PART 1

What do Trump and Charlie
Pride have in Common?

Whoever introduced this group of women to Trump, gave him the best winning strategy in the history of politics. Their melancholy mood briefly disappeared by the mere opportunity of standing on the same podium with the presidential candidate. Their agony was momentarily lifted when they were invited to come in the front. These women found solace by banding together due to their loss; they were known as "Angel Moms." Right there and then, Trumpism, had won the day by aligning itself with celestial beings, the Angel Moms. There is something peculiar about these sentient beings known as angels, whether real or fiction.

It is almost unavoidable to gossip about angels in the 21st Century. Many people believe that stories regarding angels have been with us from the dawn of human history and will never end. To my surprise, the Trump presidential campaign of 2016 had support from Angel Moms. Did you capture that moment? Do you recall that the then candidate Trump paraded Angel Moms on his podium? Were you one of the fewer people on our planet who saw that in living color? Maybe you were one of many who may have missed that exceptional moment. The 2016 campaign was uncommon and unparalleled in the history of the United States. That event followed a previous historical time, where for the first time a black man, ascended to the Oval office in 2008. Just as 2008, campaign was extraordinary in every way, and so was 2016; both were unprecedented on many fronts.

You will recall how shock waves vibrated across the world when it was announced that Obama was enroute to the Oval Office. The same melodrama played out; when the world heard that Donald Trump had won the presidency in the USA. The shock waves reached everywhere on our planet, including the Moon, the Sun, under the seas, even Trump himself. Nevertheless, that was just the beginning of utopia in postmodern politics. The best or the worst was yet to come out. It was beyond anyone's wildest dreams. It was a far-gone conclusion that Hillary Rodham Clinton would get the presidency on a silver plate. It was the greatest upset in American history. The word to describe this is not unbelievable, but unimaginable. Everyone thought that Trump was only there for entertainment, make more money and for publicity. The whole cosmos literally came to a standstill just had it happened in, 2008. These two men, Obama and Trump, were least expected to land into Oval Office, but they did against all odds. That is why the whole earth was frozen in awe because of what had just taken place! However, in my estimation, 2016 added another angle we least anticipated; the inclusion of Angel Moms, in the Trump campaign." It is not so much about "moms" but rather the association in this campaign with celestial beings, called "angels." There was a lot of gossip about Trump. Many thought that Trump was daydreaming. Other people thought he was tripping when he announced that he was running for the White House! Many politicians in both parties thought that he would be the first candidate to drop out. To some he was just a joke. Indeed a lot of people did not expect Trump to last in the race, but he did and he won? It was intriguing to notice that at every juncture, the whole world expected him to drop out. He did not. That is why the media inadvertently was glued to him and gave him free press. Trump took advantage of it. That propelled Trump to his success.

The second point to consider is how Trump used tweeter to his advantage. Trump became the "tweetiest" president in postmodern history by far. He tweeted more than all the United States Senators combined. The third point which I have alluded to is that he invoked angelic beings in his campaign (though indirectly). Let us put it bluntly; the 2016 campaign was out of this world. Would you agree that the presidency of Trump was as baffling as it was fascinating? You cannot compare Trump to any previous presidents; he stands-alone. No one has caught up with him. He is still controlling the talking points in American media. You agree that the parading of angel moms was exclusively Trumpism. Did any of you take note of that moment? Did it elude some of you? It was extraordinary on many fronts. I can predict we shall never see that campaign any time soon. The presidency of Obama and Trump are rare works of history; they appear only once in every 200 years! Mark my words.

Angel Moms on the podium with Trump

If you recall, the debates within the Republican Party was filled with innuendos unprecedented in US political system. Gloves were off; and the fight was fiercer than we have ever seen before. Amazingly, it worked for Trump. Included in all this mumbo jumbo was the invoking of Angel Moms. No other previous presidential candidate in recent history has ever paraded Angel Moms, until 2016. Besides tweeting, of all things that take place in presidential campaigns, why did Trump include Angel Moms? The involvement of Angel Moms in his campaign is what captured my attention. The invocation of celestial beings, more precisely, Angel Moms, I believe propelled him to victory. I will prove my argument further down the line. Where did the idea of Angel Moms originate? Who advised Trump to parade them on Television? Who are Angels Moms anyway? A brief background about Angel Moms who I believe helped Trump ascend to Oval Office is necessary.

Angel Moms and the Presidential Campaign

If you are a political fanatic or just a normal US citizen, you should have heard and seen the parade of wonderful women who were supporters of Donald Trump for presidency. To be precise, the event took place on

3

August 31, 2016. On this wonderful day, Trump introduced Angel Moms on his podium. Unfortunately, two men joined them (I wonder why they were there since the designation said Angel Moms) on the podium. You can download the actual event under that date above and you will see it in living color. However, the majority under that title were indeed women. For the record, Trump is not a founder of this group. Angel Moms was founded on January 16, 2001. It branched off from a small private group of moms who had connected and formed an e-mail group intended to comfort each other for the loss of their children respectively. In order to keep it private, Judi formed this group with the help of Debbie and Linda. Check this out at (http://angelmoms.com/indexpage.html.). The goal of Angel Moms was to bring together many other moms who shared "the same pain" in order for them to "survive it together.

According to the report and I quote: Angel Moms come from different occupations. They share the loss children of all ages, to different causes, and are at different stages of grief period. One segment of this group experienced loss of loved one from some illegal immigrants. End of quote. Donald Trump gave this group the biggest exposure yet. It was indeed in living color in front of thousands of supporters when the presidential candidate introduced them to his supporters. It was right there that Trump called them to ascend on his podium. It was a spectacular and smart move to garner more support for his most popular slogan, "We will build a very beautiful wall." We will make "America Great Again." Did any of you notice that, or you may have missed it? One could feel the flow of adrenalin in Trump's bones. I knew there and then that he had nailed it--his slogan and his brand! These Angel Moms ascended the podium majestically and had indeed a few poignant words to describe their heart wrenching experiences on how they lost their loved ones. It was spellbinding, "believe you me," to borrow the phrase Trump loved to use. Angel Moms articulated themselves so well; it reminded us of the Democratic National Committee moms who had lost their loved ones through gun violence too, a thing that has become common in American culture to our own shame.

We noticed for the first time that Trump at this time was no longer playing the Trump card (at least on this occasion) but rather he allowed facts to flow from these "angels" uninterrupted. These women looked majestic, austere and yet poignant without any measure of exaggeration as far as one could tell. They were real and needed comfort and there was a man who did just that. A mere display of them on public arena went very far and deep in healing in their bones. As far as I could assess, it brought a sense of closure to their sorrows. The point Trump was trying hard to solicit through this gesture, was well fastened, and the grip could not easily be undone. My mind went slightly wild; I asked myself a rhetorical question, who coined this term, "Angel Moms?" I less pondered than I wondered. It really played out well for Trump. It felt as though someone who was in penitentially had finally found his way out into the open air and begin to communicate his feelings more freely clearly. Trump knew how to win the hearts of American people whether you like him or not. Though Trump was not a seasoned politician, at least he knew his way with particular group of people. This was one of a rare tactics to score great points. Little things like this go a long way (This author is an independent. I am neither a Republican nor a Democrat). Trump and Hillary Clinton clashed with each other in this Titanic battle of 21st century. A guy and a girl faced off each other menacingly in the battle for the Oval Office. Was it a premonition that I happen to be writing a book on angels? "Can Angels Smooch" was still in its draft form when I saw on TV candidate Trump introducing Angel Moms. The exposure of Angel Moms on television was a gift to me that I decided to include in my book as it relates to smooching of angels.

Painful experience of Angel Moms?

As pointed out above, Angel Moms had their loved one's die at the hands of some illegal immigrants. That is what was reported in the media. It was a moment of comfort and solace as these Angel Moms recounted how they lost their loved ones at the hands of some bad people. It is a well-known fact that many Mexicans are good people. A few bad Apples spoil the good name of others. I wanted to dig deeper on the role of angels in human affairs. Many might agree with me that the term Angel Moms made the events more "spiritual" than political. It made my book take on a prophetic nature, if will. Interestingly, my book tried to focus on the possibility of *real angels. Can they* engage in smooching? We saw Trump *hugging* Angel Moms on the podium in living color. Is it possible to hug or smooch real angels. What would that imply? Do celestial beings participate in emotional affairs of human beings? This is one of the thorniest questions ponder in postmodern times. When did these celestial beings begin to fascinate Americans or the world at large? Can any of you recall some lyrics and movies about angels? Consider the following questions: Could invoking angelic names in your campaign bring good luck? *Would Trump have won the second term of his presidency if he had invoked angelic names in his 2020 Campaign again?* Well, think about that. I will later give persuasive reasons why invoking celestial being can be a defining moment in a person's life

Angelic Talk Never Ending Epic

I will shade more light on angelic involvements in human affairs. What prompted me to write on this topic were the lyrics I heard. I heard so many lyrics about angels. Many artists have sung about kissing angels, movies depicting angels helping people, and now we have Angel Moms in political circles. All the above points compelled me to embark on an extensive research in angelic phenomenon. What I will pen down, may sound like fiction but it is not. That is not the case. My conclusion will be based on research and personal experience. You will read certain things you have never heard before. That may make you think as mere metaphors, but it is not. If you sit back and try to think about it, you too will find them to be credible. My 25 years of teaching experience brings an indelible mark on the facts. Not to overelaborate my point repeatedly, all I am trying to point out is that I will investigate angelic puzzles as it relate to human affairs. The extensive research is necessary because these celestial beings give us a never-ending epic. That indeed begs so many questions. Is invocation of angelic beings a winning strategy? What benefits do we derive from angelic encounter? These are among many questions I will attempt to answer later on. Listening to lyrics that portrays someone "kissing an angel" preoccupied my mind for many years. I realize that these are metaphors so to speak. However, one might wonder if there are some elements of truth in lyrics and movies with regard to angels. I feel compelled to give an accurate account involving *good and bad angels*. Invoking Angel Moms, whether as metaphors or real, helped Trump in his first run for the White House. If he had engaged angelic phenomenon again, the outcome of his second presidential bid could have had a different ending. We will never know with certainty. In spite of the different results, we shall examine this thought as it relates to real stories found in the most popular book in the world. Either the good book is field with myths, but if not, we need to pay attention to it. As we move forward, let me pause and point out something essential. No one has ever photographed an angel or any celestial beings for that matter. Therefore, we do not really know how they look like. What we see in movies are mere works of human ingenuity.

Angels have never been photographed

The record still holds that no one has ever taken a photographed an angel. Therefore, no one knows how they look like. Since angels look like us, we will never be able to distinguish them from ourselves. In fact, the good book seems to affirm this assertion. The most popular book in the world states; "Do not forget to show hospitality to strangers, for by so doing some people have shown hospitality to angels without knowing it (Hebrews 13:2)." The implications in this quotation are that, angels appear exactly like us. If they appeared with wings, we would know, but they do not. To make matter worse, their Boss does not warn us in advance so that we are ready to welcome them. None of that happens. From the records in the good book, it seems that angels have visited common people lot more than they have the rich and famous. It is true that they have also visited the nobilities as well as the rich and famous. However, your station in life is not a guarantee that their Boss will send an angel to visit you. Your status in life is not does not matter. Your physical appearance does not count at all. Gender and race is out of question so to speak. The only resume delineated as necessary to anticipate angelic visit is hospitality to strangers. Somehow, angelic visit seems necessary. Even baby Jesus was visited by angels. You can see that angels are essential to our interactions in the world because they bring something special to the table even though we cannot physically ascertain who they are.

Angels were created as intermediaries between people and their Boss. The good book intimates that if you are *hospitable,* chances of being visited by angels are greater. The lyrics that imply angelic involvement with people have to be taken seriously even though they are perceived as mere metaphors. We should examine the lyrics and learn something from them.

Kiss angels

We have heard about, "Kissed by an Angel," "Kiss an Angel Good Morning," Touched by an Angel," "Angels: God's Secret Agents" "Charlie's Angels," "Angel Moms," and much more. Actually, there have been more angel interactions with humans than we will ever realize. Are there possibilities of angels enjoying human emotions and in particular kissing or smooching? Some of you may have heard or remember one of the songs composed by a country music singer Charlie Pride. Pride is a wonderful American true story to read. He is an American country music singer, musician, recording artist, performer, and business owner. His greatest musical success came in the early mid-1970s when he became the best-selling performer for RCA Records since Elvis Presley. During the peak years of his recording career, he garnered 52 top awards. One of the most famous songs he composed and delivered is called *"You've got to Kiss an Angel Good Morning* (do any of you recall that song?)." You missed out. *"You've got to Kiss an Angel Good Morning* was a big hit just after the times of Elvis Presley the icon of Rock and Roll in the 70's. Kiss an angel Good Morning. Did people realize what he was implying? Can you kiss an angel? It just dawned on this author that we never paid attention to the implications of these lyrics. Of course, they are lyrics, but is there something more to it that warrants investigation? May be it was just a few of us who would like to know more. How did he come up with the metaphor of kissing an angel? Where did he read that somebody kissed an angel? Does angelic smooching make any sense at all? If not, why then did we just dance to these lyrics so thoughtlessly? Some of us remember very well how we loved to listen to that song but did not think much about it until now. Man, that song was a hit in those days. After that, many other artists followed with similar titles alluding to angels kissing.

Another personality not very well known is Dani Bejac who wrote a book called "Angel Kissed Me," in 2010. No reaction from the public either so it looks like we have accepted the notion that angels can kiss; or we would like to be "kissed by an angel", merely "kiss an angel, "right. There is yet another artist

9

who came up with another title (her exact name is not known-but she goes by the name Noemi, from Belgium), "when angels kiss." Do you notice how closely related these titles are? "Kiss an angel good morning," "angel kissed me," or when angels kiss. That title by Pride must have been popular. I saw a book entitled "kissed by an angel trilogy," authored by Elizabeth Chandler. Susan Elizabeth Phillips did not want to be left out from kissing an angel phenomenon either. She too wrote a book called, "Kiss an Angel." Almost all of these writings are talking about "kissing" an angel or being kissed by an angel. Is there proof that angels can kiss or smooch? There are many more in the making who have referenced either being kissed by an angel or kissing an angel. Most of the lyrics above are about the positive side of kissing an angel. Well there are also some negative stories about angels and kissing. Have you noticed that some people's teeth are too bright? Maybe they were smooched by an angel. On the other hand, people who have lost their teeth may have been smooched by evil angels. You never know who kissed who

Who triggered angelic mania in the USA?

In my nonscientific estimation and academic research, the whole drama about kissed by an angel was popularized by Charlie Pride's lyrics. The person who wrote the song was actually not Charlie but Ben Peters. Charlie popularized it when he recorded it. If we carefully look back, there is no one before that who brought attention about angels kissing into the open public forum than Charlie's music of the early 70's. The good book had much to say about angels but it seems Charlie brought much attention to emotional aspect of angels. The angelic concept and belief began to take shape in the early 70's, which was probably due to the song by CP. Then in, 1976-1981, we were introduced to Charlie's Angels TV series, for the first time. What we do not know is whether that name Charlie's Angels have to do with Charlie Pride as an honor to his lyrics. We cannot know with certainty. The producers of the record can neither deny nor confirm it. And then came the 90's," "Touched by an Angel."

Perhaps in recent years most can remember the TV series from 1994-2003, called "Touched by an Angel." We know that an angel has touched some people than kissed. Touched by an angel was the longest Television exposure relating to the existence of angels in living color in our lifetime. The Television drama brought more enlightenment on angels to the public than ever before. It was one of the phenomenon of the 90's when the Clintons came to reign in the White House. What made it more popular was its focus in helping people who were in trouble. That picture of helping people must have been a reference from the good book. However, this is not my line of research I will pursue. I would like to know the angelic involvement of angels in human life on romantic level and in particular, kissing. Can angels kiss or smooch a human beings. We know from the good book that angels do not kiss each other. It is one thing to have a general interaction with people but yet another thing kiss people. Have they ever kissed a person in the past? Do angels really kiss? Are these just fancy lyrics that depict our "women as angels"? We know that the angels depicted in these lyrics refer to our actual wives we are supposed to kiss in the morning before going to work. Angel Moms being kissed on their foreheads by Trump are real people. Kiss an angel good morning we know its metaphor but could this be real? What is interesting though is that in the good book there are no female angels. Yet in these lyrics, it is women being kissed who are portrayed as angels. The people doing the kissing are males and not angels. Maybe that balances up things. Charlie Pride sung, "Kiss an angel good morning," the question is, where can one find an angel to kiss in the morning? How can you know that you are being smooched by an angel? Are angels by nature invisible beings? Can they materialize in human form so that they are capable of being smooched? Would not a kiss by a real angel be the most amazing and tantalizing experience any human being can ever fathom? Does anyone know? Who knows whether it is a holy or an evil angel that one has smooched? Let us assume that angels appear in human form as the good book often narrates to us. In view of this, how could one tell that it was a real angel or not? Bear in mind that real angels often take on human form; wear human clothing and do not appear with wings. Are there people who confessed that an angel kissed them? Here is something intriguing, angels know with certainty if they have ever kissed a person. I doubt if any of us know that without any shadow of doubt. We are then faced with the same question; is what we hear just mere lyrics without any substance to them? Alternatively, are there some truths to these metaphors? Let us read what Allison comments (in the Exorcist movie of 1975) about angels.

Allison's comments about angels

In society, in general an almost medieval obsession with demonic possession and exorcism was revived with the film, The Exorcist (originally released in 1975, released in 2000). Popular angelology could be seen in the very successful Touched by an Angel television program, movies such as The Preacher's Wife and the City of Angels, and the nearly constant appearance of books dedicated to the topic of angels on the New York Times bestseller list for literature.

In Christian literature, an example of this interest was staggering popularity of books by Frank Peretti. As recounted in this Present Darkness and Piercing the Darkness; Peretti fictitious towns are populated by hordes of demons that wreak havoc with the citizens; these people; in turn, are empowered and ultimately led to glorious triumph by heroic angels. Such tales of spiritual combat between good angels and bad demons captured the popular evangelical imagination by storm.

Evangelical theology did not escape such fascination with angelical realities. There were "numerous theological treatment that ranged from wide-eyed speculation that demons lies behind every bad habit (smoking, overeating) and sin (fornication, murder) to the concept of territorial spirits" that gain foot hold in certain geographical areas of the world and envelop those regions in particularly virulent forms of spiritual darkness (page 318, Allison). End of quote.

Notice that most of these stories and writings took place after the lyrics by Charlie Pride. In the above narrative, there is no reference to angelic kissing.

No one tried to explain the lyrics that involved kissing. Some people are being smooched even by their own dogs and cats and there is no fussing about that. It is a free world. If we just go back a hundred years, it would be an anathema to kiss your dog or a cat. People have moved away from thinking that way. One wonders what is next.

In Allison's recount above, notice that there are two different kinds of angels, good and evil. There are two kinds of people, good and evil. There are other stories of negative nature but none of them has personal backing. In our discussion about angels, I have two stories I would like to share on a personal level that may shed light on the topic of angels. The first story took place in Zambia and the second in the United States of America. Zambia is in the continent of African. The story I am about to narrate come from a far distant land. To be more precise, Zambia is in Central Africa; which is part of a larger area called Southern Africa. Relatedly, Zambia is very close to South Africa but very far from Nigeria. The story was very popular in 60's and early 70's. It took place on the Copper belt in a town called Ndola (the birthplace of the author). Many who grew up around this time vehemently believe the story to be true (how do you argue with fables). True or not, I lived there and witnessed behavior of people at night. That created some fear in me because I was young by then. The first story is about an evil angel terrorizing men in Zambia. The second one is about a stranger who massaged my feet free in the United States. Both of these stories are firsthand information.

An Angel in Zambia

In the early 1960's, there was a story about a strange angel that was going around in Ndola. This story was close to home because I lived there and was fearful to walk at night unless accompanied by an adult. This particular angel had a female name called Rose. In Zambia, if a child is named Rose, usually it relates to a female gender. However, I have noticed that in the USA, that same name can be given to anybody regardless of his or her gender. Why was the angel in Ndola given a female name? The main reason that angel was given a female name was to pretend to be a woman so that he could deceive men. The angel's goal according to the report was to ruin the reputation of men and not women.

It was well-established story that Rose loved to go out at night. The popular place she frequented was Taverns. Rose had one purpose in mind; and that was, to kiss men if given an opportunity. I had completely forgotten about the story when I was working on this book. It was the idea of smooching that brought my memories back. I lived in Ndola for a couple of years and I will try to recount what I can recall. If it is possible for angels to smooch, then that story in Ndola is the closest one I have heard about smooching. Other than that, the narrative of Genesis chapter 6 comes second. In that intermarriage of Genesis chapter 6, did the angels smooch women as well? If not, why did the obsession of kissing of angels in the lyrics originate from? These lyrics on kissing angels are not only from the USA, but also from Belgium and around Europe. It may be easy to dismiss the story in Zambia but as the saying goes; where there is smoke there is fire. The residents of Ndola were very serious when they narrated the story concerning the activities of this evil angel. However, what I find fascinating about angel Rose other than having a female name was what she was doing to adult men. Only adult men apparently were in trouble. That lessened my fears of going out at night, but not completely. Well, the kissing aspect by Rose was not mayhem to say the least. What was pernicious and intriguing, was what followed. Upon receiving such a glorious smooch, a man would lose his teeth. That is what we heard. A kiss that is able to knockout your teeth is more than a dentist work. This is where many who have heard that story begin to doubt its authenticity; I am definitely with you on that. However, if you doubt that you may as well doubt that demons exist. Read the good book and notice what demons have done to people. Do not underestimate the power of darkness as mere fantasy. Therefore, you cannot choose facts you love to believe. I lived there and my fears were genuine. Did I witness men lose teeth? No, I did not but I heard some friends telling me that they had witnessed something to that end. Living in that town was not a good thing especially at night.

Was a Zambian angel a dentist?

It is worthwhile to repeat myself; the scariest thing about angel Rose was that he stole teeth from unsuspecting men. If the story were a mere lyric like kissing an angel good morning, no one would have bothered. The story about angel Rose was different from all the lyrics we have heard. All the lyrics were positive in nature and that is why many never questioned the validity of angels kissing women. The Ndola angel was doing the opposite; she was kissing men and removing their teeth. If what was happening in Zambia had happened in the USA, many would have tried to carry out an investigation aggressively. I wonder if any media around the world heard about that story. I doubt that very much. It is unlikely that you heard about it because social media was not invented yet. In Zambia, the word of mouth and the radio where the only tools available for communications. Unfortunately, the radio in Zambia did not do much reporting. It is most likely that the Westners and the Americans missed the story. In those days, it was the era of the Kennedys. Such stories got lost in thin air in the USA. Tell us about the Kennedy's, you have everyone's attention and interested. An angel kissing a guy and knocking out his teeth was a flat joke to a Westerner. Such a story was unheard of and was dismissed right away. Unless you say lions are terrorizing people in

Africa, then a journalist may pay attention. Can you imagine someone you love losing their teeth because of a kiss? Think of your husband or adult son being kissed and in the process lose all their front teeth in thin air! When such individuals opened their mouths, red gums greeted you. Would you enjoy a smile or kiss with red gums? Only if it is coming from a baby not an adult, especially your boyfriend. Forget about smiling. Someone created a comic and called Malikope (a local slang that meant a person without front teeth) out of this unfortunate episode in the lives of Ndola people. Would you have wished an angel kissed you during that time? Not so to a guy in Ndola. It was during that time kiss an angel lyric was gaining popularity in the USA. Yet in Ndola, fear was the order of the night because there was an angel who was making men toothless. It was not only men who were scared, but women were also terrified. Most people kept indoors at night. Only the brave and courageous dared to go out alone. As you might expect, the rumor created a lot of anxieties especially when people saw men without teeth. As I mentioned before, there was no means to verify whether the story was a work of fiction or not. We had no means to check that out. Most people in Zambia are laid back and it was worse in the 60's and 70's. Recounting the story now makes it sound ridiculous but it brought a lot of fear in us then. The story lingered on for a while and I forgot about for over fifty years, until now. I came close to meeting Rose. Let me explain how it could have been possible to meet the dreaded angel in Ndola; or is it angels from Africa.

I was born in Zambia

I happen to have been born and lived in Ndola where Rose took his residence. I lived with my sister who loved life. Unfortunately, she is no longer with us. I would have loved to show her this particular segment of my book. In those days, I used to accompany my late sister (one of the courageous women) in order to baby seat one of her children while she was having a good time in a nearby tavern (a pub). Taverns or bars did not allow little children to go inside that time. There were a lot of taverns in a population of over 300,000 residents. Since there were plenty of taverns, no one knew where Rose would strike. Other than the story about Rose, Zambia is relatively a very safe country. I was less than 8 years old at the time and not yet in school. I was enrolled in grade one when I was 10 years old. Zambian weather is superb. If you have been to some parts of California, that is what Zambia is throughout the year. It is not too hot nor too cold, rainy and beautiful. "Zambia under the Sun" is the nickname given to this beautiful land. Have you heard of the Victoria Falls (rebranded-Mosi Oa Tunya), the Seven Wonders of the World? The Victoria Falls is located in Zambia. Most days are very nice and beautiful even if it is raining. In fact, we loved to walk under the rain to get a free shower from heaven. I was young and I miss that part of life in Zambia. We thought it was fun to get wet. There was no need to get a shower later at home. Some parts of Zambia are like going to Florida except that there are no beaches. Zambia is surrounded by other countries. Because of that, Zambia has no beaches and no seaports.

Coming back to my experience at night, I did not charge babysitting fees. Babysitting is usually free if you are doing it is for your relative. There were no tips to be expected either. My late sister was not married and had no job. Life was hard when I lived with her. It was during that time the story about angel Rose broke out. It did not deter my sister to go out because that is when her life became alive. The only challenge she faced was to find someone to baby sit her child at night. The next huddle she faced was that I was too young to stay at home with a baby alone. Then we received the news about the terrorist angel. Furthermore, she realized that I was afraid to go out at night for obvious reasons. But, somehow she persuaded me to accompany her. She promised to buy a bottle of Fanta or Coca-Cola. She played the game of trick or treat in order to lure me to accompany her. She preyed on my weakness. She knew how we kids in those days loved soft drinks. In those days, I longed to take a sip of that amazing thing- Coca-Cola. When I was given a bottle of Coca-Cola, it took me almost three hours drinking it! That is absolutely true! You read it right, and there are no typos. I did that on purpose and it was for my own sake. My goal was to make sure that I finished that one bottle close to the time my sister would be ready to go home. My late sister stayed inside the bar at least three hours. She was aware of my age and that the baby was with me outside. There was nothing else to do other than look after her child. If I finished that drink as I did the first time we went out, my night would be too long to bear. Next time I made sure to entertain myself with one bottle for hours. That was all I could do. I had no toys of any kind. Generally, kinds in Zambia in those days did not own toys other than play soccer. But how do you play soccer at night and with whom? By the way, only one bottle was guaranteed. As I alluded to earlier, my sister was a single mom and did not have any form of income to afford a couple of soft drinks. It was a challenge to her and I understood her predicaments. I totally appreciated her circumstances she faced. She herself depended on her friends to sponsor the soft drink and her beer. She ventured without knowing how the night might turn out. Fortunately, her friends usually came through for her. They were the ones who actually paid for my bottle of soft drinks. It was a huge gamble to go out but she was successful almost all the nights. She made it a point to go out with or without money. To her, nighttime was a time to hang out. It was very important to her to meet her friends and enjoy herself because there was nothing else to do. Some of her friends were loaded with a lot of cash. Her winning strategy was her charm. She was so good at telling stories that were full of fabrications. However, her friends enjoyed it and that is what paid her bills. There were no movies to watch. To find a storyteller like her was equivalent to watching a movie! That is why her friends loved her and in the process got away with a few free drinks. In my case while there, I devised a plan. While she was still inside the tavern, I would take my time sipping the drink on intervals. Give the baby her milk. Toss the baby up a few times and then just slowly quench my thirsty again with my drink. That was the process I went through and helped me sit there for three hours. I managed to make one bottle last the entire time she was inside. That drink also made me forget my problems not only that but also took away my fears of angel Rose. The bottle of soft drink made persuaded me to accompany my late sister in spite of Rose was roaming the streets at night. I was also comforted when I learned that this smooching angel was not interested in boys or women.

18

Things I cannot forget

The life style of my late sister had no end game. The following day my sister would come to me and say young man let us go out again (in vernacular it means, "Mwaiche tiye nakabili"). She knew I enjoyed it because there was nothing else outside our regular monotonous nshima (local name for thick porridge) that we ate with the usual greens called katapa (I hated katapa than anything else in the world other than cabbage). As you might guess, I was sold out with the idea of going to a tavern. I would imagine holding that bottle of Coca-Cola in my hands and the taste of it. Besides, I thought to myself, I would be left at home alone if I did not go. That to me was worse than accompanying my sister to a tavern. While I lived with her (for a short time), baby-sitting was the only time I had the chance to enjoy that amazing drink. After two years, I left and lived with my other affluent sister in a different location. With my other sister in a different location, drinks were in abundance. Her husband had a very good job. They even had a television set in their home in the late 60's. Television was a rare thing among many homes in Zambia around that time. It was while I was at my affluence sister that I saw and I heard Charlie Pride sing on television. Both sisters lived in the same town but different locations. However, since I was young, I could not walk to the other location. It was far. Let me get back to my late needy sister. So I used to accompany my struggling sister in order to go and taste that real thing, Coca-Cola. They used to advertise on Television in those days referring to Coca-Cola with a brief song, "It's the real thing Coca-Cola." Do any of you recall that? Do you appreciate nicer things in life? Coca-Cola of those days is not Coca-Cola of today! You may say the formula is the same. It might be, but there was no diet Coca-Cola then. That unblemished drink lured a young man to venture at night at the expense of being smooched. I had to go in spite of fear of meeting Rose the teeth terrorist of Ndola! What would you have done at that age? Stay home with no radio or Television or go out? I did what was in my best interest.

When I shared my experience with my friends that I had a bottle of Fanta or Coca-Cola; they mused; and said I was trying to exaggerate to look important. That tells you how special Coca-Cola was in those days. Life is strange; you risk it in order to take a crack at the thing you love the most. I risked my life to enjoy Fanta or Coca-Cola. In any case, it is not so much about my pop that I drank but the risk of meeting an evil angel at night. To be honest with you, I trembled most of the nights when I saw a well-dressed woman. I thought it might be the dreaded angel Rose. What strengthened me was that my sister was with me. It also came to my attention that the angel preferred older men than kissed kids and women. Not to be taken by surprise I was still on the lookout for Rose. I made sure an adult woman never tried to kiss me, not even on my chick. Whatever made my sister not get concerned about angel Rose baffles me to this day. She did not care and rarely talked about it. She heard the story. I think she believed that Rose only cared about adult men.

Now that I have matured, I think somebody was playing with people's mind and if it true, then that has to do with evil spirits. It really took many men out of taverns. Other than that, maybe someone came up with this story. That is my personal assessment. Why would someone come up with such a story? I still do not know and I have never asked anyone who heard about it. I have no evidence to either approve or disapprove it. One thing is certain; people were genuinely afraid and I saw that personally. Is it possible in our day and age that angels can smooch people? That is what I am trying to find out in my research. The emphasis on smooching swayed me and led me to narrate my short story. As you can see, this story did not have a direct impact on me. The next one did but I will let you decide what you think about it. My next story is firsthand and is every true in every sense of the word. The next story is about a stranger who massaged my feet in Oak Park, Illinois, in the 90's. The question I have tried to answer is whether an angel could massage a person. It is not smooching here, but massaging. I am not day dreaming or fabricating anything. I am explaining what happened to me in a very personal way. Angels have done incredible things in this world. We cannot limit why they cannot do.

A Stranger Massaged my Feet

Before we moved to Oak Park, we lived in Chicago for 7 years in Humboldt Park neighborhood. However, our first destination in USA was in New York. We did not live there a long time. Eventually we moved to Chicago where I went to study for my bachelor's degree as well as my masters. When the massage took place, I was still an international student working on my PhD in History of Philosophy. While in Chicago, a certain young woman came to live with us. I cannot remember the exact circumstances how we met. All I remember is that we met the beautiful young woman who was in real need. It was the first time we hosted a young white woman in our humble home as strangers. From the look of things, it seemed that her greatest need was accommodation. They were five of us in a two bedroomed apartment. My wife and our three children then welcomed her in our humble circumstances. To make matters worse, I was not permitted to work off campus as an international student. Our pockets were thin. I worked for every penny that I could get lawfully at the college. Nevertheless, it seemed that we were well positioned to meet the challenge at hand. Our visitor had nowhere else to go. I have no clue how we met. She was a white American woman with all the credentials that one of a citizen. In spite of all that, she was homeless in the beautiful city of Chicago. I was very surprised when I learnt that there were many people who were homeless. How could one be homeless in the most prosperous country on earth? As I could remember, she stayed with us for a couple of weeks (probably less than 3 months) and then she left. This was the first time I encountered a stranger. This is a back-story before the one am about to narrate briefly.

In my humble opinion there is no connecting of dots between the two strangers; I am merely recalling some things that relate to the topic of helping strangers. I know that the woman we helped was a real human being because she stayed longer than angels would normally do.

Every page I have ready in the good book, no angel has ever stayed overnight, let alone a few days. The longest any angel has ever interacted with people is less than twenty-four hours. If anyone claims that their angel lingered on for more than a day, be assured it is not an angel. Duration of time is one of the most compelling factors to ascertain whether the person who visited you was an angel or not. That is one of the acid tests about angelic encounters. As we ponder the angelic interactions and after giving you this little background, let me share with you the interaction I had with a wonderful person who massaged my feet at the gas station without charge. Two strangers, both from nowhere, one is a real human being the other is questionable.

Was I being massaged or dreaming?

I was about to pump gas in my van, a man appeared from nowhere. He massaged my feet and then vanished in thin air before I fully realized what had just transpired. That is the summary of my second story. Even before I do that let me point out something for the sake of clarity. These points will help the reader get what I am trying to communicate in the entire book. I have experienced something that is similar to the stories we read in the most trusted good book in the world. Hold on, I am in not in any way, claiming that an angel paid me a visit. Well, that might be but I have no evidence to prove or disprove otherwise. The only thing I know with certitude is that a stranger massaged my feet in an open area. A stranger, I failed to capture and remember the face! The massage he performed was stunning. I have never experienced anything like that in my entire life. He massaged my feet. Of all the parts of my body, he massaged my feet! Let me make a small confession about my feet. I have a terrible habit of walking bare feet within the house. If you happen to visit me, you are likely to see my feet with its crazy toes. When you notice them you will appreciate, how humble and loving that person who massaged must have been. If that person was not heavenly sent, then I will never know what counts as heavenly visit. To me that massager or therapist was out of this planet. I call that experience a touch of exceptional grace.

Whatever it is, it was marvelous. There is not much dram in this and I am not a dramatic person as such. The extra ordinary love I received and experienced took place in Oak Park, Illinois in the 90's. Here then is how it went down.

I remember vividly where I was and what I was doing when a stranger from nowhere met me at the gas station unexpectedly. Some of you may recall that in those days gas was as low as 90 cents per gallon. In certain areas, it was even lower than that. It was during those days that I encountered a strange man. I am positive that it was early August because the weather is usually very nice. The other notable thing is that it rarely rains in August, at least in the Windy City. Summer in Chicago reminds me about Zambian weather. It was a very nice and beautiful day when an amazing man touched me with exceptional love. A white guy appeared from nowhere when I was just about to start pumping gas. His hands made me notice the color of his skin.

An encounter with a stranger

The gas station where I brushed with the gentleman was very close to our condominium. Our condominium was literally around the corner. I easily walk to Jewel store opposite the gas station almost every day. It takes less than ten minutes to walk to either the gas station or Jewel store. I still remember the address, 333 East Avenue, Oak Park, Illinois. We lived in that neighborhood for seven years. It was at this gas station near our home that I came across a great man. He left positive emotional footprints on my life to this day. Facing the gas pump and just about to start-pumping gas, a middle-aged man was saying something to me. He was probably looking at my backside because I was looking at the gas pump. I heard an assuring voice behind me and I noticed his white hand. His voice was benign and non-threatening. The man behind me was assertive and alluring. I have never encountered a person with such equanimity, gentle, and assuring, in my life, until then. Right up front he began talking. He talked more than I acknowledged or responded. I would like the reader to get this point; I was still encroached in manners and customs of Zambian people. That is why I could not interrupt the nice guy, as he was engrossed in his talk. I was just listening but not able to see his face. I can be combative when it comes to theological issues; but social issues as such are not my thing. I am slow in socializing. My children often get surprised when I show ignorance in some social issues and would remark, "You do not know that". Therefore, when the stranger kept talking, I paid less attention. Everything was escaping me and I noticed nothing special initially. That is right; I cannot recall anything in particular about the nice man. It is one of those days when I would let someone talk and I just gobbled his word. As he kept talking about a number of things I did not understand, I disentangled the gas horse and was about to begin pumping gas. Just as I was holding the horse to the gas pump and ready to inject the gas into the tank of my vehicle, I heard the tone of the voice behind me change. I turned around slightly and came face to face with a stranger in a flip seconds. The usual "hellos" flew quickly. Somehow, without much debate I found myself sitting on the front seat of the drive's side. He continued talking removing my shoes and socks while I was sat half way inside the driving seat facing the gas pump, I had just replaced in its slot without pumping gas. I noticed that my feet where semi-inside the vehicle resting on the front seat while the stranger stooped, and begun working on my feet. He did not ask me if I needed a massage (he kept talking and I was just looking at my feet flabbergasted and lost as if I was stranded on the Moon). The space in front of the minivan allowed me to lay comfortably facing the gas pump while the stranger's face was fixated on my foot. He kept saying something to me, which I still do not recall what he meant. I said nothing all this time other than the response I gave him earlier when he greeted me. I had no clue why I was being massaged. What was taking place was quite strange. My reaction was quite strange as well. I have never understood myself to this very day. How could a stranger from nowhere make me sit inside my car, remove my shoes and socks, and then begin massaging without my consent! Whatever was happening to me at that gas station remains a mystery. It was indeed a mystery on so many angles. The obvious is that the person who began to massage me was a stranger. Furthermore, he did not ask permission to massage me. I did not ask him why he was doing what he was doing. He did not seem to care that he was doing that in an open area. What followed was efficient work of a genius in non-conversional way. I will repeat myself; I cannot remember much of what he said, not a thing other than the usual generic greetings as pointed out. First, he massaged my right foot followed by my left. I can never ever explain in words the feelings I felt in those very brief moments. I, on the other hand did not feel embarrassed. I did not resist. I did not argue. I did not respond to what he saying either. I watched myself in awe and wonder. I froze in disbelief though I did not show it. I wish it were in today's high technology; I could have taken a selfie! Is this a normal experience?

Was it a normal experience?

Now follow me carefully and analyze the events that I have just described. Here is what I know is normal; to hold a car door open for a woman so that they can get in, is normal. It is normal to hold a door open for a neighbor behind you as you enter the building. It is normal to help a poor old woman struggling to balance her stuff in her hands. It is normal to let an elderly person take your seat in a bus or train. It is normal to massage a friend's shoulders. It is normal to careless a stranger's dog or a cat if you meet on the streets. It is normal to say to a stranger "bless you" when they sneeze even if you do not know them. It is normal to wave to a fellow driver who allows you to join the lane on an intersection even though he or she had the right of the way. All the above are normal gestures we all do in a civilized society.

However, someone tell me that it is normal for a stranger, to take off your shoes, remove your socks. The stranger then begins to massage you right outside the gas station in a broad daylight! I am not so sure about you, I do not find that to be normal. Did any of you get what I just said? Should I repeat myself? A stranger came up to me, with bare hands and without gloves, removes my stinking socks, and begin to work. The massage itself had such a touch that right then began to reinvigorates my life. Mark this, there was no request, like, "can I massage your feet?" None of that emerged. Worse still,

25

I myself did not render any resistance at all. I think I am the one who is not normal. The stranger did a normal thing. Why did I let a stranger massage me in an open area without resistance? My answer is simple; I was dumb founded and froze in disbelief for unmerited favor I received. Somehow, I could not resist the free service. Something else took place; the man performed his work very fast. He followed that by his compelling self-control of his emotions. He conducted himself in his performance excellently and that is what helped me keep quiet and offered no resistance. The peace that ensued also kept me going. I had just come from the university exhausted but lo and behold, I was soothed without a charge. Tiredness may have played a huge role in my nonresistance to what I experienced. To be honest, I was emotionally drained. I mean, I was a walking zombie, and that man revived me. I know this seems unusual by any expectations, but truly, I was not myself. The therapist (massager) asked a question that still rings in my ears. I still remember the question because it was at the center of my emotions.

A question to remember

The only question that I still recall that he asked me was how I felt. I wish someone could look at my feet and my toes. I will tell you this; my feet have its origin from Zambia. That is where my umbilical cord was severed. My feet are very wide, extremely callous and less appealing even to my own eyes. I do not remember my wife ever massaging them for obvious reasons. Not even during our courtship when people are truly in love! She has never washed or cut my toe nails-not once in over 36 years of living together. My feet have the usual toes that most of us dare to look at. If I am not mistaken, I had worn the socks for three days without washing them. If you have been a student at a university, you know the experience. On top of that, I was working three to four jobs a day, what do you expect. Furthermore, I did not ask anyone to touch my feet. Get this, the amazing stranger showed no disgust at the appearance of my wide feet let alone my strange toes and stinking socks! If my wife of over 35 years avoided touching my crazy toes yet the stranger massaged them with his own bare hands right outside the gas station, which tells you what kind of a person he was. Was he a mere man? Jesus washed his disciple's feet, have you heard of that story? What is strange is that I cannot remember the man's face. I had a quick glance at his hand and that was it. He never showed any embracement at the appearance of my feet. I was the one who felt ridiculous to let a gracious man touch my stinking feet in broad day light! I do not know if any person was watching because I myself was tongue-tied and numb. I am not using these terms and words loosely. I was dumb founded and felt lost in USA because of the unusual gesture and love that was lavished on me. Get this, when I was in London, UK, people laughed at other people's toes if they left uncovered. If a Briton were to read this paragraph, he or she would get a great kick out of it. Naked toes are an embarrassment to Britons. In UK, its normal for people to stride and pick newspapers dropped near their doorsteps. Some take risks running quickly and pick up their papers without socks. Those few seconds are good enough to have a pick at the feet. If passersby see your miserable toes; my friend, you just made a wonderful day for someone. Their gossip that day will be how ugly your toes are. In simple language, never expose your bare feet before a guy or girl from United Kingdom. Unfortunately, something that made me froze happened. I happen to see the feet of one of my grandkids. I could not resist but laugh in wonder about the so-called genes. I asked an internal rhetorical question that I have no answer. Lord why transfer my ugly feet to my innocent boy? That means these ugly feet will never cease in our family. The comfort I got was that I was not the first one to introduce them. I got them from somebody. However, that somebody was created by the perfect being. On that basis I forgave myself and whoever extended that to me and I pray my grandkid will forgive me too. I add all these points to make you appreciate my experience and the unmerited love I received. You ask yourself, what kind of a man would touch such ugly feet. That is my question to this day. He never scolded or mused himself over my stinking toes. I felt embarrassed. However, I did not say, stop or what are doing. Can you believe that? I cannot believe it myself.

I have never seen a stranger massaging stinking feet of another person in an open area. Maybe if it was your great buddies, or you are experiencing great love from your best friend. I would have understood if he was massaging a woman but to do it to a man and a stranger for that matter, it is unheard of! I was shocked! I did not even thank him because I did not know his motive behind all that was going on. I felt bad after he had left that I was not appreciative. I felt like someone who had died. Hold on before you begin to think that the stranger was the scum of the earth. The stranger was by no means lost or homeless. He was not a scum by any standards. He was well dressed. His communication abilities were flawless though whatever he said swung by me because I was in the state of confusion. He was gentle. One could almost tell that his acumen was un questionable. He genuinely and enthusiastically enjoyed what he was doing. There was a lot of decency in him. I could detect it because of the manner in which he handled the whole process. If it was a scumbag, I could have known it right up front. I have travelled quite a bit and I could tell the difference. I have been scammed in three countries before, including USA. The man who was before me had no attributes of a scammer. At the end of that exercise, he solicited nothing from me. The man must have seen something in me. How did he know I would accept that favor without struggle? How did he know I would not react negatively? How did he know that he would go through the whole process in peace and without interruption? Is this how Chicagoans treat people? I have never seen it or heard anything of this magnitude. Have you had someone appear in front of your car and begin cleaning your windows? That is exactly how the whole scenario played out except there was no proper communication or payments. The more I think about it, the more confused I become. What really hits me hard was lack of reaction when a stranger was processing me. Normal people do not do that unless you are under a spell. Was I under a spell-beats me. However, I know with certainty that someone massaged whom I have never met in my life.

Recollecting massage experience

Let me reflect a little bit about my past again. I have already mentioned that I was born and lived in Zambia for 34 years. No one has ever massaged my feet. My brothers and sisters have never done that to me not even my mother. For the first time a stranger massaged my feet. I have never seen a person massaging a stranger's feet outside a gas station. I call this act ion, a massage of heavenly touch and nothing short of that. It was exfoliating and invigorating at the same time; and the result was fantabulous. Such things are performed either in parlors or Spas but not at gas stations. In one sense, I trembled when I reflect on the experience. What was happening to me? Who was that man that poured his soul on me at a gas stinking place? I truly felt touched in my innermost being than ever before. To be honest with you, I was very scared when it was over. You may wonder why such a thought entered my mind. The answer is very simple; I was an international student and very broke. I feared that the stranger was going to ask me for a fortune in return for the work he had performed even though I did not solicit it! Not a word from him concerning any payments. There was also fear in that the therapist was going to propose to me. I lived in Oak Park. Oak Park is one of a few suburbs in Illinois where there are a large number of gay people. I was already married. There were many partners in the condominium where we lived. To my surprise, none of my fears was realized. There was not a whisper of a request of anything. He never extended any such gestures. Well the least I expected was that he was going to give me a business card as an invitation to pay him a visit at his business center. That did not happen either. To my surprise and before I knew it, my socks and shoes were meticulously replaced and lo and behold he was nowhere to be found. He was gone before I could even say anything.

The gentleman controlled everything from the beginning to the end. I do not know what happened to my mind, I feel as though my brains were frozen, I could not think. I am not that slow either. He was gone, literary gone with the wind! Who was that fellow? I have no clue to this day. Do angels smooch? What about do angels massage?

My "angel" disappeared

As I was going through this process, on one hand I was puzzled and yet on another I felt like I was daydreaming; I was literally tantalized. Was I in the spirit, trance or just daydreaming? Was this really happening to me in real time and space, or it was all about clairvoyance? I knew it was not telepath because I was able to drive home by myself. When I bounced back to my senses and numbness the stranger who had done all these wonders was nowhere to be found. It seems to me that I was frozen in disbelief and fear because I said nothing and asked no questions at all. He vanished in the same way he appeared. He was nowhere to be found anywhere I could look. I did not see him massaging other people anywhere near the gas station. Just like that, he disappeared in thin air. Yes indeed vanished. What is even more amazing to me is that I have never told this story until now. I am literally re-experiencing those emotions as I recount that incident. I have never told anybody on this planet until now. I just remembered that experience when I began writing the story on do angels' smooch. I was not entertaining strangers. I was being entertained. When I flash back, as I usually do, I began to ask myself questions, why did I not offer to remove my shoes and socks. Why did I not offer to put them back-trust me I was spell bound so that the whole process begun and ended by the will of a stranger. This is a true story of one of the chapters of my life. It took place in the 90's in Oak Park of Illinois. Somebody lovingly massaged my stinking feet and as I write about it, I feel so good, appreciated and loved. It was a marvelous thing to be touched by special love especially from a stranger. Strange as it may sound, that actually happened to me. Can someone help me out here; do you know how my feet felt? The massage was performed with precision and it produced amazing emotions. Whoever he was, he knew where to touch in order to produce the needed results. The massaging was a pure work of a high caliber professional. It worked and produced wonders in me. I appreciate what professional massagers can accomplish in a stressed person; I was one such a person. People who know their work can a make lasting impact in the lives of others. Some are in this business to make quick bucks. Others are in it for their legacy; this man was in it for the sake of other people. He was a genius at massaging, and he did it brilliantly.

The first thing he did was stroke my feet and toes by using his knuckles. I have never seen professional therapists use knuckles as a tool to massage. He pounded his knuckles around my feet. He was as gentle as a sheep and as patient as a crocodile. Then secondly, one by one he caressed each toe. Using his fingers laboriously, he found his way gently into my toes in such a manner that made my brains relaxed. I felt intoxicated with soothing when he drove his two fingers between my toes with such precision that left me wonder what he was driving at. It was an instant healing of the dead body. When he had done that, he looked at me and I looked away immediately. His massage was so therapeutically designed such that my fatigue instantly disappeared. I am ignorant of the study of reflexology, if anything; this man was a genius in reflexology. I could have gone to see a chiropractor, physical therapist, massage therapist among other professionals but I wonder if any of these experts could have brought out what the stranger did in very few minutes. Then, finally, he applied the usual technic. He put my feet slightly on the seat of the car, elbowed up, so that my feet rested on the seat. He then put his thumbs underneath my feet. Then he began pressing them firmly while moving them about. As I said before, until that moment, I have never been massaged by anybody in my life at all. It was as if I was tranquillized, but without the use of medicine. It was a mere work of a master therapist.

I know my experience may not fall under entertaining angels, but I could have been the one being entertained. Whatever it was, I felt touched by fingers outside our universe. Something touched me for a purpose. Something good descended on me with immeasurable favor. Is there a reason I may have received this favor? I am not sure but I cannot recall any special work I did to warrant the special favor while I was in college. The only inkling of kindness was assisting that woman who lived with us for a few weeks. We were not expecting a pay back. It was a joy to help a stranger in need even though we ourselves were strangers in the then great city of Chicago. Surely, you would agree with me if I ask some obvious questions, who massaged me? I have reached in my senses and realized that the stranger left heavy impressions in me. I remember more of what he did than how he looked like. I can recall most of the details of his work than how he was dressed. What kept lingering in my mind is the question of massaging my feet and not the shoulders. Why massage my feet, and not the shoulders? I could not find an answer to the hard questions. I recall when Jesus washed his disciples' feet. Peter then suggested having his whole body washed-that is what I am thinking now. I still wonder who massaged me. Good things came out of the experience I went through. This incidence gave me renewed vigor and energy I had never expected it. All my ligaments and sinews were reborn in a sense. I knew I could go on for the next year as though I lived like a normal human being. Like a river, I felt rejuvenated! The help was tremendous that came at the hands of master massager. The performance coming from somebody I had never known made it something unforgettable. Was someone ministering to me in order to give me new strength as I labored on my PhD that was giving endless headaches? I wonder if I will ever get an answer to my question. Maybe it may help to reexamine the encounter.

Analyzing my encounter

Now about that person that touched me, I cannot remember the shape of his head and he had no beard. He had no strange clothes. He had a normal human voice. He had no strange accent except other than a pure Midwest American accent. I know he was a white man from his hands and a quick snapshot of his face. I do not know if he was driving a car or not. I did not see him come and go. He just appeared and then vanished. I am looking backward to see if I could remember anything special. As I have said before he did not give me a business card or a cell phone number, (cell phones were not that common in the 90's). We cannot even talk about the physical address for that matter. I am beginning to wonder whether I was momentarily in a dream at that moment or dementia may have crept in. I wonder why I forgot to ask for his name. My incognito visitor did not volunteer to give any of his credentials either. What I learnt from the experience and from is that it is not up to human beings to plan for the angelic visit. That would make us plan and receive them appropriately. Unfortunately, heavenly visitors do not work like that. They direct the course of every action in every way. Perhaps that is one of the annoying experiences that we do not like about spirituality. We are used to controlling everything we do. No one has ever photographed celestial beings: We do not know how they look like. Whether my experience was angelic touch or not, one thing is certain, I went through an exceptional adventure of my life.

We know that many people have received heavenly visitors at one point or another. None of them expected that visit. I would like to give example of such individuals as we move on. That is our discussion in part 2.

PART 2

Benefits of Interacting with Angels

I am convinced Trump would have won the second term if he had included Angel Moms on his podium again. There is something about angels that mesmerizes me, their ability to transform themselves instantly into humans. Based upon my research, I have concluded that *when a good angel* interacts with an individual, they always bring amazing blessings almost all the time, with very few exceptions. That is why I think Trump won the elections the first time. *There was no way he was going to win.* Even he himself knew that. The second time he never paraded Angel Moms and he lost in spite the fact that he was the sitting president. *The invoking of celestial being directly or indirectly almost always brings tremendous benefits to an individual.* Angel Moms were unknown. In the first campaign, Trump lifted their spirits by emphasizing with their painful experiences. To Trump it was just a winning strategy. To these women it was a huge comfort to their loss. What does empathy do to a person? It lifts heavy burdens and instils hope. That is what happened on that day. Just a mere touch from a public figure changed their lives. Forget intentions by Trump (most politicians use photo ups for their gain). These women felt loved by that exposure. It is a good thing to do. To me it is one of the rare gestures that I ever saw Trump execute even if it was for self-interest.

Let me ask a trillion dollars question: Does the inclusion of celestial beings guarantee supernatural blessings? What would happen if a real angel were to touch or smooch a person? Let us reinforce the question; can real angels bring good luck to those who interact with them? Before you dismiss the point as mere works of fiction or daydreaming, we should check the facts from history. I submit that majority of my arguments will be based on the stories from the good book. To that end, if you do not trust information found in that book then my points are invalid. I have confidence that the good book speaks the truth. From my research, I discovered that anyone who had some association with good angels have had their lives changed. They were not the same persons as we used to know them. Trump did not have real angels. That is why his luck ended when he did not include Angel Moms in his campaign again. It seems that we have not done enough studies in the role angels play in human affairs. Especially as it relates to emotions and sexual activities. Is there any evidence that some people have been smooched by angels? Answers to these questions are a few pages away. In addition, we will try to find out why angels mingle with people incognito. How come hosts of heaven do not disclose themselves tell us right away that they are angels. Why hide, why the camouflage? Do you realize that we are surrounded angels every day? We are, and they perform a lot of work oblivious to us. I hope the points I make do not shock you. Most of us have heard of a few lyrics that suggest kissing angels. Now we should include Angel Moms on that list. Have you heard songs such as, "Kiss an Angel Good Morning?" Well, many more are still coming on the market and our work is to analyze a few of these lyrics. That is what I am doing. You see, science works from fiction and ends in reality. So too spirituality works in lyric and ends in reality. Research does not end; it is an ongoing process in the spiritual as well as in the material world. Let us look at Angel Moms a little bit more.

Reflecting on Angel Moms

As I have stated above, we have heard many lyrics about angels. Angel Moms seems to be the one of the latest addition. There may be more we may have missed. Angel Moms obviously were not real angels, as you very well know. However, the presidential candidate hugged these moms. As far as I am aware, it is the only group of women carrying an angelic name to be hugged by a presidential figure. They were kissed on the cheeks or forehead (not sure) and it was quite an emotional scene. I did not see any smooching. These women experienced excruciating pain; hence being hugged or kissed on the foreheads in public felt like a healing medicine. However, I cannot resist keep asking the same nagging questions: Have real angels been smooched by human beings? Alternatively, have human beings smooched real angels inadvertently? Even the suggestion of these questions leaves many feeling creepy. Trust me, I am meant it. The good book does not hide anything; preachers do. Preachers sometimes try to paint a rose picture, which the good book is not communicating. Our depraved minds, not the good book, make us feel as if such questions are detestable. The majority and reasonable people will agree that angels have certainly mingled with humans on numerous times even though we have no physical evidence. Nevertheless, I still wonder if somebody has witnessed an angel giving a smooch to a person. Who is likely to initiate such a move? *I will lay down some steps that angels take when they come and meet people.* No one seemed puzzled or confused when we listen to lyrics that depict angels being kissed because we know that its metaphors. However, I would like to go beyond mere metaphors because the good book seems to imply otherwise. Have real angels smooched people before? Are these just fantasies and mere works of fiction we have dreamed about? That maybe so; but the questions are quite serious and deserve investigations. We have heard so much about angels and their interactions with people before. That has happened throughout world history. From antiquity to the present. It is an endless phenomenon. Have you by any chance been smooched by an angel? My personal experiences I had in Ndola of angel Rose maybe questionable to some. I have now realized that there are many things we still do not know. The only way to be sure is to investigate. We have to have spiritual scientific mindset. Search the Scriptures and figure out what we still do not know. That indeed is where the rubber meets the road! Come along and let us dig meticulously into the affair between humans and angels. Let us hit the issue heads on. I promise I will leave no stones unturned, but you are free to leave some pages unread, you decide. We shall investigate every possible activity in which these angels might have been involved. Why not start by reexamining the work of angels among people. What does history reveal, or the good book teach?

Reexamination of work of angels

One of the goals we are trying to achieve is to reexamine the work of angels in their interaction with human beings. Among other things I will investigate is angelic wardrobe. Is there such a thing as angelic wardrobe? By the end of this book, you will know that angels have wardrobes. We shall find answers to the following points; where angels get their shoes, clothes, socks, hats, and many more stuff that is necessary to make them look like us. What happens to these outfits once they get back to their heavenly home? In addition to analyzing lyrics, movies, books, we need to examine the narrative in Genesis (Genesis 6:1-4). Is this a credible story or its just myth? Were the angels who married women good or evil? Did they really indulge in the immoral behavior stated in that narrative? Did they smooch and inadvertently impregnate these beautiful women in the process? Do angels really exist and appear as male humans, or it is just a figment of our imaginations? If it is true that angels are real and that, they relate to us; do they affect elections in our world? We have heard the lyric "Touched by an Angel?" How factual is that statement? What effects do touched by an angel accomplish, if any? Have angels touched someone in real life? Angels are life changers and they are not far from us, look out.

Angels can be life changers

Angelic phenomenon is a global belief. We have all kinds of stories around the world attesting to the existence of angels. Some people said that they have seen angels. In Russia a "Mind-blowing Story of Russian Cosmonauts Who Saw Angels in Space (source: Mission Galactic Freedom). In Islam, the belief is that "angels are naturally obedient creatures, worshipping Allah and carrying out His commands. Angels are genderless and do not require sleep, food, or drink; they have contingent free will. However, those that decided to side with their Boss live in total obedience to Him. The Quran says: They do not disobey Allah's commands that they receive; they do precisely what they are commanded"(Quran 66:6). In the religions of the East, the function of angels in Eastern religions was carried by avatars, bodhisattvas, and other such spiritual beings that were extensions of God or the sacred. Beyond traditions of different cultures of the world, there are literally millions of personal stories of how certain people feel that an angel helped them. The closest book to the Judeo-Christian Bible is the Qumran. The Qumran is the religious literature that contains certain names of angels who are also found in the Bible. Take names such as Michael and Gabriel, these two names are found in the Qumran as well. That means these two names among angels are well known. However, the Qumran also contains specific angels with specific duties. Here is a brief list of some angel's names and their duties:

1. Ridwan-Guardian angel of heaven
2. Israfeel –The trumpeter angel to mark the Day of Judgment.
3. Mikail – An angel obligated to the flow of rainfall and sustenance.
4. Munkar – An angel question people about deeds and faith.
5. Malak Am-Maut -These two are known as angels of death.
6. Malik: He is the guardian of hell.

When it comes to naming, the Qumran surpasses the Bible in that category. Nevertheless, when it comes to detailed information and the activities of angels, the Bible comes up on top. The critical issue is how far angels have been involved in the activities of human beings. How far do they go when it comes to romance or human affections in general?

The Qumran and the Judeo-Christian Bible are arguably widely read and respected spiritual books around the world. If you put these two books together, billions of people around the world have heard something about angels without question. I will focus on examining the Judeo-Christian Bible as it relates to angels and people. Most lyrics in Western culture about angels rely heavily on the Bible. The lyrics we are familiar with usually insinuates angelic kissing (kiss an angels' good morning). What type of kissing do we have in mind when we sing such songs? If angels are entangled in human emotions, is there a possibility that people may have been kissed, or even smooched unknowingly? Is being touched by a good angel a sign of blessings? If you say no, my question to you is; why do most people who have had contact with good angels seem to prosper in life? Conversely, those who encountered evil angels live in big trouble. There is more information from the good book that seems to support such conclusions. Is that book fake or real? As one reads from the good book, when a good angel visited a person (as we shall see) their life was never the same without exception. Their lives changed for good or ill but never the same again. There has been amazing transformations in many lives. Let us glean at a few known cases from the Judeo-Christian book. I am sure the Qumran has examples too.

People whose lives were changed because they met angels

Gleaning from the well-respected book, we discovered that people who were touched by angels became famous, rich and well respected. For example, Abraham is one of the (from the Bible) popular names in the world. When did that happen? That name was unknown before; it was until three angels visited Abraham that his fame was established. Things began to change for Abram (who later became Abraham) after a real angelic encounter. Abraham among other things became one of the richest men of his day. Many babies around the world are named after him. Consider this; Abraham is the ancestor of both Jews and Arabic people (father of Ishmael and Isaac, both have become among the largest religious groups in the world). To this day, the Middle East is one of the wealthiest places on our planet. These blessings were the result of angelic encounter by Abraham. If you consider Abraham's brief history, his fame began to grow when he was told to leave his parents. Afterwards he received a surprise visit by three angels. That point in history was transformative to Abraham, whose family were idol worshippers. Not only has Abraham's fame increased among Jews and Arabic people but his respect has also expanded to include many religions including Christianity. I believe his fame went even further and include some great philosophers as well. Some philosophers have debated endlessly the narrative in the Genesis account of chapter 22 regarding

Abraham's willingness to sacrifice his son Isaac. In a crude way, Abraham is indeed a father of many nations not just in Israel and Middle East, but also across the globe. After being visited by angels, his name later changed from Abram to Abraham a symbol of success and many blessings. Where did the fame of Abraham originate?

Abraham and the three angels

As we have argued, Abraham became famous after angels visited him. His life was revolutionized. The visitation by heavenly hosts became a life changer for Abraham and his family forever. Wait a minute, yes; it included the change in the history of the world. We should also point out that visitation by good angels is the most powerful event that any person can ever fathom. However, what is even more astounding if not overwhelming is the fact that whenever a good angel visits a person their life is never the same! If a mere encounter could bring immeasurable benefits, what would happen if an angel were to touch, kiss or smooch an individual? Would that mean the blessings would double? We ask again the same ever-enduring question; do angels smooch or they just render an angelic kiss or none of these emotional things? What about the lyrics we hear or read about, why have we not questioned their meaning? Is there truth to these metaphors? I would like to know whether in real life angels have entangled themselves in human emotions. We shall examine good and evil angels in (evil angels in fewer details) their relationships to people. I will briefly try to make a contrast between good and evil (demons and Satan) angels. Let us develop the angelic and human interactions by citing a few more examples from the good book. If you have read the most popular book in the world, you will notice angels have "touched" many lives. I will include those who were touched by angels but not in a chronological order. I have picked names at random just to make a few valid points. However, some events in our discussion are well-established stories even in other literature.

Mary and an angel

Another famous name to consider is Mary, the mother of Jesus. Mary engaged to Joseph. An angel paid a visit to Joseph regarding Mary his fiancée. At that moment, Mary's name was unknown. Mary's status was changed when an angel visited her. Not only did her life change but also her place in history changed as well. For starters, her name became a blockbuster of all time among female babies. According to some reports, "over the last 100 years, the male name Michael has held the top spot most often (44 times), while the female name Mary has been ranked number one 40 times over those years." Virtually every nation around the world has had at least a female baby named after that name. Not only that, Mary is venerated by the Roman Catholics religion to the point of being worshipped (they may deny that). There is no evidence that she was kissed or smooched by an angel. Mary is held by many as a representative of women before the Boss of angels. Ask yourself, which name among women would you even dare to compare to that of Mary? Maybe her cousin Elizabeth can come close. We ask the same question again; when did Mary's name gain popularity? The answer is simple; it began when she had an encounter with an angel.

Among women born on our planet, Mary received the most gracious words ever given to any woman. You can read for yourself the book of Luke chapter 2; it is a masterpiece. She had nothing to do with that personally.

Angels' impacts on the life of Mary and Abraham

When did Abraham and Mary's names begin to have an impact on the world? Catch this, just like Abraham; Mary was unknown until she met an angel. Both Abraham and Mary were absolutely nobodies--really nobodies. Let me remind you something very important again just in case you missed my point earlier on. Abraham's parents were pagans who worshipped idols. They were unknown by any standards. They were engrossed in pagan activities just like many other people in their country. There was nothing positive that warranted Abraham to be a recipient of the heavenly visit. Nothing qualified that man to gain access to angelic embracement. Mary likewise, was just a simple woman who was pledged to be married to unknown man in Israel. She was just going about her personal business like many virgins in her city. There was nothing special about her virginity compared to other women. The point is this; she was not the only virgin. That translates to mean; virginity was not what qualified her to gain favor from angelic visit. There were many beautiful virgins like Mary at that time. Her name was unknown until an angel visited her. Observe something else. Neither Abraham nor Mary was from a royal family. Notice very carefully; Abraham and Mary each came to fame when an angel paid them a visit. There was nothing special for either of them to deserve angelic visit. We know that someone superior to them sends angels. They do not act on their own personal whims. That means their Boss sends angels to visit people on earth. To be visited by an angel, is an indirect way of being visited by God himself. That is how special and important angelic visit is. That also implies that these angels come with the full authority of their Boss (the Sender). The point is that, there is something exceptional when one meets an angel. Another name that comes to mind is Mary's cousin, Elizabeth, who gave birth to one of the most famous names on our planet; namely John the Baptist. Until John was born, there was no such name known as John before. Today the name, John, is everywhere. I will talk about John later on. Let me make few points about Elizabeth, the mother of John.

An angel visits Elizabeth

The name, Elizabeth, is among the most popular names named among the Royal families of Great Britain. Elizabeth became famous indirectly through her husband Zechariah. An angel visited Zechariah. Unfortunately, Zachariah paid a heavy price for doubting the message brought by an angel (one of the rare negative news brought by angels). Why did he pay a heavy price? Zachariah paid a price because he should have known better being a member of the priesthood unlike Mary. Mary too if you notice, questioned the impossibility of giving birth without having a man. She was not punished because she was not a member of a high class like Zachariah. Never the less, grace was extended to his wife. That visit by an angel to Zachariah gave birth to a man named John the Baptist. According to Jesus, John was the greatest man that ever lived. John is another household name among male children around the world (especially the Western culture). John baptized and introduced Jesus to the world. John was the son of Zachariah whom the angel visited. These are stories you have heard. Have you noticed how they are linked to angels? Angelic connection is their source of all the blessings (they come from their Boss of angels). We are not done yet, there are some more examples to be cited.

If we look back and examine every person visited by a good angel, you will notice that their life thereafter was never the same again. Even TV series Touched by an Angel, gives us positive feedback when they encountered an angel. It is not being presumptuous to state that an individual received good things after angelic visitation according to the good book. We can even go back to antiquity and look at the life of Hagar, for example, the servant to Abraham who received a visitation by an angel of the Lord as she was running away from Sarah her boss.

Hagar and an angel

There is fascinating stories among the giants in biblical history. One that relates to Abraham and his family. We read that a quarrel ensued between Abraham and Sarah regarding their housemaid, Hagar. Abraham said he had nothing to do with it. That was a cop out by a great man. Instead of resolving issues, he avoided to lead. Same thing happened when he went to Egypt. Not to excuse Sarah, she is the one who brought Sarah to Abraham so that they could have a child. Now she is blaming her husband. As you could see, family feud have a long history in the world. The one who thought had won the jackpot was the maid. Unfortunately it was short lived. The housemaid realized that her position had improved. Somehow after the child was born began showing off. When Sarah saw Ishmael mistreating Isaac that infuriated her even more. She complained to her husband. Abraham just said do what you want with her. We know what happened; Hagar was booted out of the house together with her only son, Ishmael. She left the household of Abraham and went into the wilderness. There, alone with a small boy, came face to face with an angel. An angel provided what Hagar needed for her son and herself to survive. Hagar was then told to return and humble herself before Sarah.

That moment of Hagar meeting an angel in the wilderness was the greatest turning point of the life of Ishmael. Hagar's seed (Ishmael) was promised to receive material blessings from Abraham' God. The majority of Hagar's seed has occupied the Middle East to this day. Notice what has become of her seed; the Arabic nations are one of the richest people on earth. Some may not like the truth but facts stand before us. She is the mother of Arabic people to this day. The father of their posterity is Abraham the same father of Israel. Jews and Arabs are related through Abraham and Hagar. It is critical to hold the truth in check; the wealth of Arabic people cannot be attributed to Muhammad, but Yahweh the God of Abraham. Their riches are from the God of angels, the God of Abraham, Isaac and Jacob. Before Muhammad was born, Abraham was and became the source of all their material possessions. We know that the rival between Jews and Arabs began with Sarah and Hagar. When women are upset, the world pays the price. We are witnesses to that rivalry to this day. No one would be able to separate the rivalry between these nations because their war is anchored on their common ancestor. Their rivalry is from antiquity of which few people on earth will never understand. Observe a great distinction; *what made the difference in the life of Hagar was not Abraham but the angelic visit.* Abraham had nothing to do with Hagar coming back to him. Abraham had nothing to do with the wealthy Israel would inherit' God made that promise through an angel (Genesis 17:20). She came back and her son inherited the material blessings because of the angelic visit. Notice something important, there was nothing good about Hagar to receive the blessings that were promised to her posterity. Those blessings began with that angelic encounter. I am not making up these stories. If the good book is believable, then we should pay attention and we are not done. Another example many people have heard about is Jacob, the grandson of Abraham.

Jacob and an angel

Another biblical figure we know too well is called Jacob (grandson of Abraham). He too became well known after an encounter with an angel. Jacob's name was changed to Israel. His name became the name of a nation we now know as Israel (means prince) even today (Israel is a brand name). Without controversy, Israel is one of the most well known countries on earth (besides Egypt in Africa, which is the oldest known biblical name in the world).

You can imagine how monumental that encounter of Jacob and an angel. What we know a country by that name, came about because a conniver met an angel. Israel was founded when a man named Jacob fought with an angel. Jacob specifically asked for a blessing, and he received. It was indeed one of the greatest blessings anyone before him had ever received. Maybe with the exception of his grandfather. In another crude way, Jacob was a swindler. Jacob was a thief and had run away from his brother Esau. He could not give free food to his brother who was hungry. He refused to share food with his own brother who was dead hungry and now he is the recipient of one of the best blessings in the world. Was that love or what? Instead, he tricked him in order to get something from him. He is like Cain who said am I my brother's keeper. He exchanged food for a birthright. He swindled his brother of his birthright by using food. Jacob wanted to be on top of everything. After that, he agreed with his mother to steal his brother's blessings. In other words, he connived with his mother and lied to his father that he was Esau. My point is obvious; there was nothing meritorious about Jacob. He was not even his father's favorite if you know the meaning of that in that culture. All these points worked against Jacob. Things changed when he encountered an angel. The conniver's name was changed to a prince overnight because he struggled with an angel. Everything began to fall in the right place. Even his older brother he swindled showed him favor. As one can imagine, we are not overstretching the angelic encounter at all. I am trying to stress my point by giving many examples so that you get the point. The man who robbed his own biological brother (actually twin) twice became the prince. When did that take place? It was after an encounter with an angel. Analyze this; what was the difference between Jacob and Esau in human terms? Both were flawed in their own right. There was nothing worthwhile for Jacob to be favored as such. Somehow, the life of Jacob was changed forever while his brother remained miserable to this day. Jacob became more than a prince; his name was elevated to be the name of a nation. That name is called Israel. Israel means a prince. Israel was the new name for Jacob. Clearly, that came about after meeting an angel. We can add many more names, but let us add to the list the name that is greater than all the names I have listed so far; the name of Jesus. Very few people around the world have never heard the name of Jesus. On my final illustration on the impact of angels, let us focus on the name of Jesus.

Jesus and angels

Christ is not the earthly name of Jesus. That is his official title. Christ just means anointed. In other words, Jesus is anointed. The name Jesus is his human name or more properly earthly name. It is a relatable name to us. It is a human name, our brother in a sense. In that case, we are his earthly brothers and sisters. He was born, learnt to sit, claw, stand, walk, speak, and eventually was able to run. He was human and needed human protection in his infancy as a man. He was born in peculiar circumstances than the rest of us. He was born like Adam with direct breath from the Holy Spirit and yet was carried inside a womb of a woman. That was necessarily so that he was attached to us as we were with Adam. When he grew up, he was assigned with the responsibility to bring an end to sin that came through Adam. Later on, he was anointed and that is why he bears the name Christ. The Son of God does not need anointing in his spiritual form. As a man, Jesus was born in challenging circumstance. When He was born, he was placed in a manger (where the cattle fed from. Notice, he was not born in a manger but was placed in a manger). At birth, he was surrounded by stinking stuff where he was placed. Jesus (like John) was a strange name too. No one had that name in Israel before. The people wondered why Joseph and Mary would name him as such (it shows preeminence of Jesus. He stands first in everything). Again, Jesus is his natural earthly name as a person. The only people who truly believe that the name Jesus is an earthly name are Mexicans who name their children as such. Other nations are scared for no good explanations. Mexicans make Jesus a real human person. Their theology on that point is impeccable. It makes Jesus human like any other person on earth. On the other hand, the term Christ has to do with his ministry to people and not angels. The substitutionary doctrine works well since Jesus was a man. You have to have faith in Jesus and *not in Christianity*. Only Jesus saves nothing else, not Christianity. The truth is found in Jesus not Christianity. It is critical you understand the distinctions. Jesus himself proclaimed that he was the way the truth and the life. You cast demons out in the name of Jesus not Christianity. Jesus saves not Christianity or Judaism. How do angels relate to Jesus then? At his birth, an angel appeared. Then a group of angels appeared to the shepherds and announced his birth. I hope my readers captured that thought. Many angels came to sing praises but also to inform expectant people of his arrival.

We can see that as a human being, Jesus was not excluded from having angelic visitations. In his Godly form, angels were always available in his presence without having to wait for them to appear. In his human form, they had to appear at certain times. At one time Jesus had one angel appear before him. Later many more angels appeared to the shepherds at night in Bethlehem to announce the fulfilment of his birth. At another time, an angel appeared after his temptation by Satan. Why angels even the Son of God? Angels are the representative of God. Even human Jesus needed that. Tones of angels that appeared at his birth were already on earth. Shepherds saw them with their own eyes. Jesus began his ministry after the temptation by Satan and ministry by a good angel. Holy and evil angels visited Jesus on the same day. From that time on, Satan never tempted Jesus in a big way. Billions of books around the world have been written in the name of Jesus. Thousands of church buildings are named after his name. Many have become rich through his name whether with good or ill intentions. Thousands of preachers have become famous because of him. Movies have been produced under his name. We cannot even begin to talk about the number of songs that have been written bearing his name. The Roman Catholic Church is famous because of the name of Jesus and Mary. Jesus had thousands of angels attended to him on many occasions than any human being ever born on our planet. It is very logical to conclude that angelic visitation has powerful ramifications and brings amazing benefits. Angels guided Joseph and Mary to go to Egypt in Africa. This is real stuff. Jesus was no exceptional to angelic visitation! Think about it with a sober mind and put aside religions including Christianity. Do not boast about Christianity, but about Jesus. None was called a Christian, from Adam to John the Baptist. No apostle called himself a Christian, but a disciple, or servant. The church in Jerusalem was called the Way, not Christian. Many of these people will be in the kingdom of God. They had faith in God. My point is that people have misunderstood Christianity. There is no salvation in Christianity. There is salvation in Christ. It is very important that you get what Jesus taught, go and make disciples, not Christians. If people call you a Christian, it is all right. That is what happened in Antioch, where people called believers, Christians. They did not name themselves as such. Abraham and Noah were not Christians but believers in God and will be in heaven. Let us now consider the benefits that accompany angelic visitations. We have pointed out in general that certain people received immeasurable benefits after having contact with an angel.

Angels and blessings

The point I am laboring to make is this; you are likely to inherit lasting blessings if a holy angel were to visit you. You will join a class of distinguished people that have ever lived. If that were to happen, you will never be the same again. The lingering question before all of us is; how do I know an angel visited me, since they usually come incognito? That is a trillion dollar question! It is an emphatic question. How do you know that an angel visited you? The good news is that there are hints recorded in the good book and a few outside it that can affirm that you had an angelic visit. We need to begin to unravel our everlasting conundrum (quandary).

I am aware that much has been written and discussed concerning angel's entanglement in human affairs. It is an assertion that is broadly accepted that angels have participated in human affairs. What we are not sure of is whether they are deeply involved in human emotions as well? That is another huddle to disentangle. We shall face these questions as well. I have cited many examples of the power of angelic visit. Let me give you some hints that can help you know that an angel may have visited you.

Some signs that an angel may have visited you

Is there any evidence to prove that someone may have entertained an angel at some point? You may have been at home, in a shop, at work or any given location when you received unexpected visitor. The two words, visitor and stranger, will be important in our discussion. You may have a visitor but they are not necessarily strangers. How do I know an angel may have visited me? The general answer is that, if a stranger interacted with you less than a day and afterwards you received lasting blessings, that is a good sign that it could have been an angel. Here is the difference. I talked about a woman who was a total stranger and lived with us for some time. That woman is definitely not an angel. Angels do not linger for more than a day. I am actually stretching it. Usually if it is an angel, twelve hours is well too long. Only in exceptional circumstances, have angels stayed longer but even then, is always less than a day. That is the first clue. Anyone who is going to claim angelic visit and such a person stayed more than a day, are lying. The visit you may receive might be at night or during the day. Ask yourself the following question; how can one be certain that the person that was entertained last night was not a mere human being? Then follow the simple procedure of self-analysis: First, think and look backwards and examine past events that you went through? Secondly, recall how things have been in your life before an encounter with a stranger. Thirdly, examine how things have turned out after that encounter. Caution; make sure that you do not force issues. All you need to do is face the facts before and after the visit and then draw some highlights. However, do not draw conclusions yet.

It is critical that one follows these steps. Here is the most important point to keep reassessing within yourself: *Look at your life before and after that visit*! The second general principle is to compare your experience with the examples above. Consider their lives before and their lives after the encounter. Compare that to your own personal experience. Now get this; the changes must be extraordinary and should last the test of time. *We are not talking about a few great sweet moments in your life but powerful noticeable extraordinary changes for you and those around you. That would last your lifetime at the minimum.* That is the test before you make any conclusions.

The procedures and points above are very critical and necessary in ascertaining the truth of your experience. These points can help anyone come to logical conclusions. The points are well scrutinized and researched in history as well as the Scriptures. Something uncommon and extraordinary will happen to you without exception if you personally encountered an angel. The change maybe gradual or is instant, but it is always remarkable and lasting. It has happened and it is still happening even as the book is under way. How do we know that? The experience of people, literature and the most trusted book can testify to that. This is not guesswork or cheap talk, but a reality anchored in facts. If you are hospitable, you may qualify to have an angel visit you. You can also know for sure if you follow the steps, I have articulated above. It is also true that a good thing have happened to people who never encountered an angel.

We know that angels are not the only ones who may bring great fortunes. However, such fortunes, that are purely natural in their nature, cannot compare to fortunes angels may bring to people. We should realize that people who encounter angels are not necessarily religious. No one is guaranteed to meet an angel, not even true believers in God. Remember, Abraham was not a worshipper of the true God. Jacob was not either. Even Hagar was not. Yet all these individuals were blessed beyond expectations. However, there is a difference between the fortunes that arise due to angelic associations and the natural ones. Mere earthly fortunes usually are for this life alone. However, angelic fortunes incorporate the heavenly and earthly life. Can you capture the difference? In the present life, there are highly talented and gifted people who may help turn your life around in a big way. Some of you may win a jackpot that would bring you wealthy least expected in your life. Money can definitely change your status instantly in this life. It is not only money. Fame has its own rewards in the present life. In our world, we have seen amazing minds that have literally changed the trajectory of world history. There has been revolution upon revolutions that has captured world attention. The pace at which the 21st Century is moving, will definitely transform our world into something un imaginable. Leading that race are people we call genius. The exceptional minds have literally affected not only our world but also other planets. That means the entire universe is at the fingertips of the gifted people.

We need to be careful those of us who claim religion or faith about what we say regarding people who are making amazing impacts in our world. Therefore, whoever mocks nonbelievers is shortsighted. Wisdom informs us that gifts of God are irrevocable. That means God gives talents to all his creation pagans or people of faith. We need to remember that nonbeliever in their human natural have affected each of us personally even some may deny the existence of God. Take for examples, non-believers who are medical doctors. Medical doctors and nurses have saved millions of people in their field. Add other professional such as pharmacists; just these two professionals have helped billions of people across the globe without prayer. Physicians know how the body works. Pharmacists know how to interpret the dosage of medicine you need than a bishop in your church who also needs their help.

In spite of their denial of God, you cannot deprive them the help they have rendered to the human race. We have to be thankful in general that even non-believers are driven to the pursuit of happiness and excellent work.

Whoever denies that lacks the knowledge of the Bible. We do not depend on miracles daily. We depend on natural talents that God has distributed equally to all his creation. Some doctors are believers and so are some scientists. The role of Popes, bishops is to guide people in the realm of faith. They are not superior to any other professionals. We have to give credit to scientists and researchers who want to improve our world. Do not focus on their personal pursuits. Religion has been one of the greatest hindrances to progress. Just because someone has a title clergy, does not make them knowable on how things run. That is the greatest lie that we have ever been told. The Bible clearly says respect all people including all categories of leaders. If the world were left completely in the hands of religious people including Christianity, we would still be living in the Stone Age. Whenever Christians do not like what nonbelievers are doing, they hide in the name of God without facts. Most people who are bankrupt on the knowledge of true God flock mindlessly to popes or bishops (bishop is the same word that means pastor). That is what I mean when I said we would still be living in Stone Age. People need to be smart and use their mind God imbued in their minds to examine what is true and what is false. Religious leaders are the greatest manipulators of people followed by political leaders. Our Creator has given us amazing talents as human beings.

Having said that, there is a big difference when it comes to the work of geniuses and angels. In almost all the cases, geniuses have to deal with *material blessings or tangible stuff!* As you well know, we are living in postmodern world where the speed of technology is unparalleled in the history of the universe.

In spite of the tremendous inventions and the miracles of science and technology (science, not scientists, is not in opposition to God), still, angel visitations is far superior to any modern achievements. That is a critical distinction to highlight. A real change in a person has to affect the *internal* and *external* disposition of a person. Put it bluntly real change should affect the whole person; that includes spiritual and material blessings. To deny material blessing is a lie. To deny spiritual blessing is a lie too. God made both and gave them to human race. I have discovered that in every single case found in the good book where a good angel visited a person, their lives were never the same again spiritually and materially. Sometimes material blessings by people visited by angels are latent. Here is a simple explanation so that some readers may not miss the point. Sometimes when an angel visits a person, there is no apparent tangible proof. Unless some of you do not believe in after life but if you do then my point is firmly established. If there is another side of to our world, then there is an entrance to it. Let me put it another way; angelic visitation has *eternal* consequences than material blessings. No matter how rich a person maybe, if they lack faith in the invisible God, once they die, their life is over forever. However, that is not so to someone who has had angelic visitation. An encounter by an angel may affect a person beyond the grave. An angel received the poor man Lazarus while the rich man's wealthy did not continue to bless him while in the grave. Someone even asked; what would it profit for a man to gain the whole world but loses your own soul? That does not translate that wealth is bad. It just means prepare to have both. Say, you are a billionaire; do your billions equal to how long you will live? Alternatively, you are one of the geniuses that changed earthly life, does your ingenuity carry you through to a better life. I hope the reader gets the distinction between angelic visitation and people who have blessed us with only material stuff. These two points are not on the same level at all. I am very thankful to the great minds of our day that have helped us make life easy on so many fronts. Human minds are exploding in ways we have never known before. As we speak, USA has attained another amazing stride. On 21 March, USA landed a spacecraft on the surface of Mars. They left a drone that is able to take photos and send them to us. How far is that from us? That is over 300 hundred million miles away from our earth! Going to the Moon is no longer a feat.

Entertainment industry has reached reaps and bounds unheard of 30 years ago. Our children do not know what toys to play with. My grandkids ages, two, four, and six. They know how to play electronic toys that I cannot figure out, let alone engage them. They look smarter than I do by far! What else is missing in terms of our comfort! We were able to come up with a vaccine in less than a year. We have devices that we use in social media that makes you think you are in the same room with a person in China. A person in Africa can watch Netflix in their home as if they were in Chicago. We have blockbusters upon blockbuster almost every single day. These and much more have changed the world. Buying food or clothes is no longer an issue. Just press the button and you get what you want in a few minutes. With all these devices available at our fingertips, one would think that everyone would be smiling every second, right! Not even close! Why not? With all the modern achievements have we not yet reached utopia! What is the problem? It is very simple, we have improved only one area of our lives at the expense of another; *our internal* world has not changed. Not even with the availability of medicine. Watch this; it is the external world that has been changed drastically, with leaps and bounds. The curse unfortunately has entered into churches that have joined *political* systems. What a tragedy that people who are supposed to be the salt and light of the world are using political lenses to judge other people made in the image of God. That is the greatest curse in our postmodern times as far as faith is concerned. Infact judging from behavior, a person who belongs to the same political group is well received than a true believer. The label they have established are destroying the faith and guess what, they are blaming nonbelievers instead of examining ourselves. Friends, we who claim faith are destroying the world because we align ourselves to political systems. It is not just claiming your faith; it is righteous practicing your faith that matters before God. I truly applaud human achievements in very way. Unfortunately it is one sided.

Our internal struggles (HUMAN HEART) remain the same since we became humans. For example, hate has not changed. Envy has not disappeared. Murder still runs in our blood vessels. Lying is the order of the day. Cheating is a common theme. Jealousy still makes us commit murder. Coveting is a game even babies' are guilty of. Greed is exploding than never before. Selfishness is a disease that makes us worse than animals. Racism, tribalism, and caste system keeps running in circles. Hypocrisy is the greatest sin of clergy and politicians. There are more vices such as; resentment, malice, bitterness, deception, slander, gossip, the list is endless. War and rumors of wars have their source in the hearts of people and that is why we are still at war. You see the external world; the world of our mind and perception is becoming amazingly wonderful while our internal world the world of our hearts and feelings is getting sicklier every day. You know all that. I am just putting it on paper. No matter who you talk to, our internal world have never improved since humans became humans. Our inner dispositions are getting worse by the day. It is impossible to please human beings; accept that. Divorce is worse in our day when we have plenty and easy access to what we want. Trust me; the external world cannot solve the issue of the internal world. Material cannot replace spiritual. We need both. Both do not mean going to church and singing wonderful melodies. Both means our inner dispositions matches our external dispositions. In other words, do not just say no to abortion and fail to boycott killing races you do not like. Religious people act like that. You are not a true believer just because you hate that one particular sin. If you break one chain, you break them all. That is what Jesus promised NOT Christianity. As long as hearts do not change, utopia is a pipe dream. Can you reconcile these two poles? Can you see the quandary we are facing? Ability to change the material world is half the answer to our quandary. If our internal world were changed first, it would be very easy to attain utopia in the external world. Wars and everything else in the world begin from our internal world. People who have experienced internal change and had external material stuff, have the possibility to experience the best possible world. However, an angel helped every person who had that experience. Abraham is a good example. That is why when these strangers visit us; they bring in something we cannot produce by merely using human ingenuity. So again, angelic encounter, is one of the blessed hopes any person can ever fathom (remember, good angels do not come in their name-but in the name of their Boss). Let me give a few more clues on how to know an angel visited you.

More clues that an angel visited you

One of the best indicators that you may have had an angelic encounter is that your life will forever be different. It will be different in every way. The best proof is to look at the examples we cited above. Jacob who was a thief and conniver became very humble later in life. We pointed out even his name was changed to a prince. It is not so much about wealth but the quality and longevity of life itself. That is the most critical point in all realm of angelic encounter. There are extremely fewer cases where angels may tell you outright that they are angels. The angel who visited Zachariah for example made it clear. When they do this, it is usually in visions but in case of Zechariah and some women who went to the tomb, they appeared in human form. Usually angels maybe disclosed to that person after they have delivered their message. Visions are helpful points in which you can tell that an angel visited you but the problem with that is that it is just a vision not the physical person present with you. In our day and time, it will be a real angel in human form who will visit you. Again the best method we know that a certain individual had an angelic visitor is a *change life*. We are talking about big change, a change that extends and affects other human being. To encounter an angel would bring drastic changes in your life. Nevertheless, how can you position yourself to have access to angelic visitation? That is where the rubber meets the road. That is what we shall discuss next.

Three Options of Having an Angel Visit You

There are at least three possibilities of an angel visiting a person. I will draw attention to the third category. The first one is unpredictable because it falls under the prerogative of mercy. The next two points are conditional. (1) Unmerited mercy (2) Care for the Poor (3) Hospitality to strangers. Of the three, the most likely to have angelic visit is hospitality to strangers.

Unmerited favor

Un merited mercy (favor) is whereby you receive a favor from the Boss of angels for no reason. An angel may visit you out of the kindness of God. What do we mean by "unmerited favor from the Boss of angels?" By that statement, we mean that the angels' Boss could pick on any person in the world and bless them. We may call the action, prerogative of mercy. Un merited favor does not require any action from the beneficiary. It is given without reference to the character (it doesn't matter whether you are black or white, short or tall, rich or poor, religious, famous or not) of the recipient. The angels' Boss can show mercy to whomsoever he chooses without merit. We have many examples on this. People like, Abraham, Jacob, Hagar, had nothing going for them to receive heavenly favor. Recall that Jacob was still a conniver when he had an angelic encounter. Moses was running away as a murder when he had an encounter in the burning bush. Other virgins in Israel and Rome could have been chosen than Mary. All of these people received mercy without merit. In our day, unlike in Bible times, unmerited mercy is very uncommon. It is hard to rely on that possibility. God can still do it but it is rare. No one knows why God conferred mercy on certain people. We do not know when he will do that again. Unmerited mercy can be given to believers as well as non-believers alike. It has nothing to do with religions of the world including Judaism, Christianity or Islam. Let us remember that these religions were not in existence during the life of Hagar, Moses, Jacob, Joseph. This is beyond general mercy the Boss of creation pours on earth like the Sun, air, rain and much more.

On the other hand, God gives general mercy to us in terms of basic things. He does even expect worship in return. A person can still choose to worship him. It says "I will have mercy on whom I will have mercy (Romans 9:15)." It is a general statement and we should take it as such. An angel would be sent to a person to deliver such a favor. Now the difference in this particular mercy is that it is usually in material form and but not in spiritual (many have become believers by choice after receiving mercy but not all) form. It is important to take note of that. General mercy or unmerited favor are un conditional. A case in point is the story where Jesus healed ten lepers. Nine went home healed and Jesus never forced them to believe in him. Only the Samaritan came back and gave thanks to Him. Jesus did not require him to do so but he did. That is the same case of Abraham. He was chosen by mercy but became a believer and was later named the father of faith. We do not know about Hagar or Naaman (the commander of the Syrian army). However, they too received mercy in different ways in proportion to their needs. We can give more examples but what we have is sufficient to make a point. The point still stands; God's mercy is unpredictable because it is up to the angel's Boss to execute it. He can give it to anyone he wants and expects nothing in return. In short, it is not a reward for doing anything good or bad. It has nothing to do with salvation. Mercy that has to do with salvation is called grace. That kind of mercy (grace) requires a willingness to respond. It is not given to a person who won't respond. Mercy (favor) can be given without expecting a response. For example, healing a baby. Salvation cannot be given to a baby because it is incapable of response. That tells you that there are different kinds of mercies. God can offer you a gift to save you from sin, but you must accept it. He cannot act arbitrary to your will. Mercy (favor) is different. The execution of mercies involves angels. He sends his angel to you to give you his mercy. He alone decides without your consent. God can heal you without asking you. All these activities are done through intermediaries (angels) except salvation. We move to the second point on how to have angelic visit.

Care for the poor

Care for the poor (similar to hospitality but slightly different) that comes from a pure motive (not out of the sense of duty). In this scenario, you have played a role to be a to recipient of angelic visit. In this scenario, you played a role. However, God is not obligated to give you anything special. He is just rewarding you out of his benevolent heart. In the one we just discussed, you never played a role. God just picked you from nowhere. The second means of favor is not guaranteed but it is a position of a possibility, if God so desires. A good example is a man named Cornelius-a Gentile not even a Jew received angelic visitation because he was kind to the poor. The angel specifically stated," your prayers and gifts to the poor have come up (Acts 10:4)." In other words, his sincere care for the poor earned him a favor from above. However, that favor is not guaranteed to all who care for the poor. That is a very important distinction. It is likelihood but not an obligation on the part of God. We see that in case of Cornelius. An angel visited him. His family and his friends earned something greater in life. He became a believer and even his household joined him. Tabitha is one of the few women who was very generous to the needy. When she died, she was raised back to life by Apostle Peter (Acts 9:36-42). This may not have involved angelic visit but the apostle Peter alone could not raise the dead, the Boss to the angels was involved. Her love to care for the needy with a good motive gained her favor from the Boss of angels and her life was given back after she had died. Do you suppose her life will be the same after coming back from the grave? The third point is the most important because it affects us more today. Whether you are a believer or not it still affects you. In spite of what you have heard, you qualify to have angelic visit even if you do not believe in God but as long as your hospitality come with a pure motive. Some religious people do not like this truth, and I still do not understand why. Are you genuinely a hospitable person to strangers and not the people you like? It is easy to be hospitable to a very beautiful woman and vice versa. There is a motive there and you have failed the real test.

Hospitality to strangers

In postmodern world, being hospitable gives you the greatest opportunity to garner a visit of an angel. This is a stated principle that has happened before and continues to happen around the world. It is open to any person not just believers (pagans, Jews, Christians and any religious person). Here is what we read from the good book (writing to Hebrew believers but giving un open statement) "Do not forget to show hospitality to strangers, for by so doing some people have shown hospitality to angels without knowing it." The author is very, very concerned and quite emphatic about it, "do not forget." Then he says "some people" have already entertained angels without knowing it. He did not say some believers have. He said some people have. We ask a general question, who had a chance to entertain angels in the past? People who were hospitable to strangers. It does not say believers but "people." We must accept a general statement to stand by itself without forcing the meaning. It is not special people, but people who were hospitable.

For example, Cornelius was not a believer when he showed hospitality people. Because of his generosity, an angel visited him. Fortunately, he later became a believer himself and so did his family. What we can take from the Scripture is that it is possible to receive an angelic visit if you are truly hospitable. According to the good book, even Jesus talked about a stranger. For example, in the account of Matthew, Jesus said, "For I was hungry and you gave me something to eat, I was thirsty and you gave me something to drink, I was a stranger and you invited me in,[36] I needed clothes and you clothed me, I was sick and you looked after me, I was in prison and you came to visit me (Matthew 25:35).' In the book of Romans, an injunction is issued: "Practice hospitality (Romans 12:13)." Peter adds and says, "practice hospitality without complaining (1 Peter 4:9)." There are more. All hospitable people, pagans or otherwise, have an equal chance of being visited by an angel! This is the truest statement ever stated! The only people who may not like it are some religious people. Religious affiliation is not the guaranteed means to receive visitation by angels. Practicing hospitality is. Religious people are expected to be hospitable, but few are. Usually if you are hospitable, it is to those of your kind and expect something back. If you behave like that, an angel will never visit you. It says strangers. They may not even be believers but mere strangers. Believers can also be strangers. However, if you have a genuine hospitable heart, it does not matter who you help.

Hospitality to strangers is rewardable

The third point is the only one that comes with a command. It is not always that everyone who is hospitable will entertain angels automatically. Nevertheless, hospitality is the only act that is commanded that comes with the possibility of meeting an angel. In other words being hospitable puts one at an advantage to receive the blessing from the Boss of angels than any other means. It is predictable because the person who coined that is the Boss to angels who does not lie. This is not guesswork; there is likelihood that it will happen according to the good book. The imperative states, practice (continuous doing it we do not know how long. just make it a habit) hospitality to strangers. If you do, you may end up entertaining an angel. It has nothing to do with being a pope, pastor (bishop-same word as pastor or overseer), deacon or any ministerial office. It is an open imperative to any person. The imperative was directed to Jews but it is an open imperative. Some people entertained angels without knowing it. He tells the Hebrews to do that so that they also may have an opportunity to entertain an angel. However, it is open-ended imperative to any believer or pagan who may adopt that attitude. It is not restrictive at all. There is no classification except you practice hospitality continuously. An angel can visit any person on earth if they practice hospitality to strangers. Strangers are people you do not know. The strangers might be visiting you or your neighbor.

The three points above are the clearest paradigms of angelic visitation. The good book seems to indicate that any person has an equal opportunity to have an angelic visit with positive results. The first one depends entirely on God himself. The second is conditional based on care for the poor. The third is an injunction that carries a greater chance to entertain an angel. There is a fourth point but it negative. An angel with negative consequences may visit you. You really do want that to happen to you. Negative consequences generally stem from extremely bad behavior. My goal is to encourage you to open your mind to the possibility of receiving a visit with positive consequences. As such, I would like to dwell on positive encounter for your well-being. I will revisit the third example with more points to reflect on.

Consider this; *good angels do not come empty handed.* Your hospitable attitude may have led you to entertain an angel at some point in your life, without knowing it. You may not have realized that. All you see is that your life has drastically changed. You may not even trace the roots of your changed life. The issues we are discussing are very significant. That stranger you welcomed in your home, happened to be an angel, and he did not come empty handed. That visit will change your life and will not be the same again. Let me repeat myself; good angels do not come empty handed even though they pretend to be strangers. They always bring with them good news. There is no story in the good book where an angel was sent to punish a person who was hospitable. There is absolutely nobody in the history of our world! It is always positive and full of good things that follows that individual. We gave some examples above concerning a few that were visited by angels. All of them without exception had their lives changed forever.

People, and in particular, believers are encouraged to be hospitable. It is true that there is no guaranteed a good angel will visit you. Yet your chances are greater if you are hospitable than if you are not. On the other hand, it helps to live a life of anticipation because you never know when your turn might come. Besides, we should learn to do good without expecting a reward. We are not talking about fake angels with wings. We are talking about angels who look like us. How do these angels infiltrate our companies? Let us examine how these angels will mingle with us incognito.

PART 3

Common Practices of People and Angels

There is a lot we share in common with angels. They have wardrobes just as we do. I would like us to compare manners and customs of angels to people. Let me say it upfront, there is none. When angels in human form while on earth, they adopt manners and customs of any culture under the Sun. In simple terms, angels are enculturated. We share common practices with angels. They do not act contrary to the traditions of their host. If we all understand the point I just made, it will go a long way in understanding the behavior of angels while among us. I will draw attention to their clothing and necessary accessories that angels would use, while in human form. In other words, I will spend less time discussing particular food they love to eat (let me reveal a secret, they eat anything the host puts on the table). Earthly clothing gives angels the best camouflage. Dressing in human attire, enables angels to blend in amicably. Garments make it easier for them to mingle with earthly entities without detection. We are not talking about guesswork or mere conjectures, but practical activities that make angels elusive. They hide from us so that they are able carry out their mission effectively. A word of caution; do not waste time hiring the CIA or the FBI to figure them out. FBI or CIA cannot figure out angels by applying human methodologies. The best technique of investigations that CIA or even FBI may utilize would not work against them. Even if the whole world hired investigative branches such as; FSB (Russia's equivalent to USA FBI) or other great probers, such as Shin Bet of Israel or British M15, or SO15 including their special branch, it still wouldn't work. My point is that, nothing under heavens can detect angels among us. Angels are greatest spies and masters of evasiveness on our planet. They know every activity-taking place on earth, and yet we cannot even detect their presence. Having said that, let us consider how the whole scenario plays itself out. I said earlier, my emphasis will be on their garments (Angels do not appear nude nor with wings- that is Hollywood fiction). The phrase I will spend much time on is the following, "entertained angels without knowing it." That is s phrase in our debate.

How is it possible to be with someone who happens to be an angel and yet fail to recognize them as such? What would that mean? The logical answer among reasonable people would say, the strangers among us are very good at assimilation. In a sense, angels are special spies that adapt the traditions of the world in order to infiltrate it. Angels have never been caught. However, human spies have been caught several times. To this day, no one has caught an angel and say, oops, I got you! Why have people failed to unmask angels throughout history? It is simple; angels are genius at camouflaging. They have mastered our practices; they dressed like us, speak our language, eat our food, respect our norms and observe our traditions and practices. Would any reasonable person argue with that assessment? We know that angels have been entertained a million of times since the world came into existence. What constitutes entertainment? Each country has its own set of rules that define what entertainment entails. So if these beings were able to go around the world and got entertained appropriately, what would that mean? The only logical conclusion is that the strangers were able to fit in. It means they understood traditions of any given nation and acted fittingly. We have been informed that some people have entertained angels without knowing it. It is not a question if it may happen, it has already happened. In addition, we are further informed, the angels will be entertained in the future by people who are hospitable. The reason angels have never been detected is that they are very good at blending in. It takes good planning to camouflage your identity. What is the purpose of traveling incognito or camouflage? The answer is obvious; to accomplish your goals without being discovered who you are. Angels come with clear objectives in their minds that they would like to achieve unnoticed. What makes people fail to unveil the identity of angels? I will list a couple of points below regarding angels:

1. First, we must agree that these strangers do not come nude.
2. Second, we must agree that these strangers appear already dressed before they mingle.

3. Thirdly, we must agree that they participate in all activities their hosts are performing.

4. Fourthly, we must agree that they do not disrespect their host.

5. Fifth, they observe traditions and cultures of their hosts.

6. Sixth, they strangers do not have wings.

7. Seventh, they have the same normal heights of regular people.

8. Eighth, they do not intimidate their hosts.

Whatever angels do in any country or city they enter, they do not give a hint or suggest anything that could reveal who they are. Since angels are international emissaries, then it follows that they can blend in every culture of the world. With these few observations, we have captured what to anticipate. What I will lay down should not be difficulty to understand and follow. I will describe particular outfit they may use in order to blend into any particular group of people they visit around the world. However, before we go there, I would like to mention one or two points regarding their IQ. Angels come "incognito" and that is their MO. The word incognito comes from the Latin word 'incognitus' meaning 'unknown' and later adopted into English from the Italian word incognito. That is the proper operative term here throughout the Scriptures. Furthermore, these heavenly hosts are extremely intelligent. How great is their IQ? How can we measure their IQ? Only by illustrations are we able to appreciate their IQ.

Angels IQ is superior to people

Let us remember that angels are extremely smart, sentient beings. One angel is smarter than all the geniuses of the world put together. Think of the best well-known genius individuals who has ever walked on this planet, then, and now-they are better than that by far. Think about this: They know world affairs100 percent. They have unmatched experience in worldly affairs. They know everything since the world came to be. To add icing to a cake, their Boss who lives in heaven is the source of all that we know and shall ever know.

Angels know everything that we do on this planet as well as other planets. They even know what we love to eat individually. They know all the cultures of the world. They can speak any given language of the world. They do not need interpreters because they are linguists by experience. They can easily win elections because of their vast knowledge of human behavior. No, they are not omniscient, but they are more knowledgeable than all human beings put together. The point being made is that when it comes to ingenuity, angels are in the class of their own. They are exceptional brilliant entities the world has ever known. Angels amass billions of experience of human affairs. They have seen it all. The longest person that has ever lived is less than one thousand years. At minimum, each angel has more than twenty thousand years of experience of watching human behavior. Twenty thousand years (is a very conservative number). One angel has that amount of experience to say the least. In addition, angels are very loyal. They do not deviate from their goal. We can testify to that when they come and perform certain duties on earth.

Angels operate under commands

Angels follow orders all the time. They are commanded where to go, when to go and what to do. They know how to behave themselves before any group of people. They dress according to the expectations of that social group. If, for example, an angel were to visit the late Mother Theresa, an angel would dress up according to the taste of her company. Angels would make sure to buy clothing suitable for her circles. If on the other hand an angel were to a visit to the pope, they would dress up in violet, white, green, red, gold, black, rose lines for holy men of cloth. That way, angels would look like bishops or the archbishops of the Roman Catholic Church in. Angels will make sure that they blend in with wits and wisdom to be accepted as normal human beings without any hint of suspicion. Another example; if they were to visit the Masai of Kenya in Africa, or some Zambians in a village, they would dress up just like them and communicate plainly in the local language. In other words if they were to visit our world, they would assume the total package of human expectations.

No one has ever said to an angel, I know who you are, unless an angel personally gave clues to that individual. Angels are linguists. They know all the languages spoken on earth. They are fluent in all the accents of the world. Their Boss created all human languages and their accents. He must have them. They will wear sandals like those that they did when they visited Abraham. Sometimes they will walk bare feet if the hosts are without shoes or sandals. They will wear boots if the locals love boots like Mexicans. They will wear hats like cowboys to make life easy. They will even join in singing popular songs with the locals if need be. That is part of their incognito interaction. They will do anything under heavens to infiltrate, be accepted, and carry out their objective. Knowledge of manners and customs of a particular group of people is necessary to angels. Speaking in local dialect has happened before. That is why people who spoke to angels thought they were talking to their fellow nationals. It is possible that you may have spoken to an angel and you thought it was just another person. An angel who spoke with Zachariah made it clear to him that he stood in the presence of God. Why did he say that? He said because Zachariah doubted the message of an angel. The reason he doubted is that the angel looked like any Jew in Israel. He was dressed like them and spoke their language. I am sure you are wondering if they appear already dressed. If that where the case, where did they get the attire? That is what I would like to focus on next. Where do angels likely to get their stuff they need while on earth. There are no shops in heaven. The residents up there are all spiritual beings who do not need material things. Spirits have no need to wear anything. However, when they descend to the earth, they are already well dressed. Have you ever wondered where they get these normal human apparels? If angels were to dress up contrary to human expectations, it would defeat their purpose of incognito. They purposefully appear in human garments in order to conceal their identity. If they were dressed like creatures in Isaiah 6, most people would run away. All angels who come to earth are well dressed because they come to deliver important information. The knowledge of the language of people and manners and customs of the world, gives angels ability to interact with people. It would help to look at their outfit more closely.

Angelic outfit

You probably are wondering in your mind; what kind of clothing and shoes are angels likely to wear? Ask yourself, what kind of clothes do you think angels would love to wear when they visit people like you? Would you expect them to wear fancy clothes, as the Britons would have us believe? Can angels wear designer clothes? If you are rich and caring, you may have given clothes to a stranger. Look back, who was that person you had a chat with last night? If you are hospitable to strangers, you may have entertained an angel as well. Let us emphasis what is obvious here, no angel has ever appeared nude when they visit people. Real angels have no wings and do not appear nude (except Hollywood angels). Almost all the angels we have read in the good book come already dressed in appropriate normal outfit. The only exception is when they adorn themselves in their special tailored shining clothing. However, special clothing is reserved for very special occasions for example, the resurrection.

We know without any shadow of doubt from the good book, movies and other narratives that angels appear already dressed. I have never read any narrative that has portrayed angels appearing nude. In other words before they descend to earthly, they make sure they adorn themselves with the appropriate outfit. The clothing's they wear are real. Everything from their perfume and hairdo are well done. In real life, no one has ever reported having seen an angel flying with wings. That would be obvious. It is only in visions or dreams that one could see a flying angel. In real life, no one has been able to see an angel flying with wings and then landed at a house. These are not just stories we have made up; they are based on the most trusted book on the planet.

Angel's outfit plays an extremely important role in their mission. Where then do angels buy the stuff they use? Since they use genuine earthly clothing, sandals, and other necessary outfit, where do they get them? These angels have eaten food cooked by women like Sarah. As far as Sarah and Abraham were concerned, the three visitors were real people. The couple did not seem surprised when they came to their tent. The three individuals looked like men. Abraham was not startled when he saw them. As per tradition, they offered these three men food and drink. Common sense tells us that the clothes and sandals these men were wearing were not out of place. Human hands must have tailored the garments these men wore. Here is my point; whatever these three men were wearing, they were made on earth somewhere. The stuff they had did not originate from heaven. We may not know exactly from which store they got their stuff, but whatever they used, was manufactured on earth. Sarah and Abraham saw angels eating earthly food, but they never saw them buy clothes or sandals. If our observations above are correct, then we assert human hands made the clothing they wore. That tell us they got the stuff from well regular earthly stores. That demands fair investigations into the source of their attire. Recall what we pointed out earlier; these angels blend in well in any given culture. That means they do not wear the same kind of garments everywhere. What are the likely places or stores where these visitors buy their outfit?

Where Angels Shop

Now look, do not think too hard, angels get or buy clothes anywhere normal human beings would. There you have it. They buy stuff from any shop or market. That by the way includes special stores where you can buy designer stuff. Angels knows every Mall in the world. Here is what is likely to happen; before they descend to our planet, they plan where to go and shop. They know exactly which store carries a particular brand they need. Bear in mind that angels are persons. Therefore, these heavenly hosts sit down and plan what they need and where to get it. They are well organized and their communication system is flawless. If for example, a perfume was needed, that would be included that on their checklist. Angels are not omniscient but because of their great organizational skills, they know almost everything going in the world. They meet and discuss among themselves and share their knowledge. Sometimes they help each other fight battles (Daniel's book-10:13). In addition, their Boss (who –knows all things), can furnish them with details they may need in no time. On top of that, each angel has thousands years of personal experience in worldly affairs. That is possible because angels do not die they are spirits. We are right in assuming that angels have been to almost all the shopping places in the world. That includes all the Malls found on our beautiful earth. That brings us to a critical question; how do they decide what particular fashion wear on their mission?

Angels are fashionable

Let me state a very important point; angels choose their outfit based on whom they will visit. Without any shadow of doubt, we can assert with indubitable knowledge that angels get and wear any brand of clothing that is appropriate. The point being made is very critical because it plays a big role in their mission. The determining factors in what to wear are the class of people who they intend to visit. Nothing eludes these hosts of heaven. They are well versed in the latest fashion of shoes on the market. The new line of clothing. The high quality jewelry and distinguished perfume. They know the brand names of what is popular or fading. I gave a few examples above what kind of fashion angel would wear on a given trip. Let me expand the list. The caliber of a person an angel will visit determines what kind of attire to wear and where to buy them. For example, if an angel were to visit Mary the mother of Jesus, or Elizabeth her cousin, Wal-Mart's (there was no Wal-Mart during Mary's time, it is just an example) lines of clothing would do. They know Mary's lifestyle and circumstances; therefore, anything from Walmart will be just fine. Neither Mary nor Joseph was rich. Anything you may get from Walmart will be appropriate for her. On the other hand, if an angel were visiting a woman in Kalindawalo village in Zambian, who is impoverished, anything from Salvation Army or salaula (used clothes) would work. An angel would also make sure to adorn himself with all the trappings of a villager in order to fit the occasion. That would make them welcomed as equals in a village. It is not the goal of angels to frighten their host. That would disrupt their mission. Remember there are there to accomplish something not as pageants. That is why they dress up appropriately to suit the occasion. We know that some villagers are extremely poor and may have no shoes. Angels will make sure that they go without shoes. In all literature I have come across, angels have frightened their hosts less than five times in the history of the universe. The only time they seem to frighten their hosts is when they dress in their shinning clothes. We should realize another important point; angels do not decide the person to visit. Their Boss does that. Once they have been dispatched, they know where to go and what to do.

As we pointed out above, the determining factor depends upon the social group they plan to visit. There are different brands of clothing that are popular in each given country. For example, in **France,** we have the following popular stores were the rich people prefer to shop:

Christian Dior
Givenchy
YSL
Lacoste

Popular Italian brands
Armani
Dolce & Gabbana
Ermenegildo Zegna
Prada
Gucci
Diesel

Popular USA brands
Thom Browne
Ralph Lauren
Tommy Hilfiger
Calvin Klein
Levi's
J crew
Club Monaco
Abercrombie & Fitch

Some Popular British brands
Hackett
Paul smith
Ted baker

Some Popular Germany brands
Hugo Boss
Marlboro Classics

Each country has its own distinct shopping areas where to buy their stuff. In almost every country, one would find dozens of used clothing stores as well for the poor and those that are struggling in life. If one were to travel to India, China, Africa, Japan or Korea you will find that they too have particular stores for the rich as well as the poor. Here is what is fascinating when it comes to heavenly hosts; all the above stores; whether it's for the rich or the poor, angels shop from any place depending on who they will visit. They will shop from any of the above store depending on where their ministry will take place. For example, if an angel were to pay a visit say; Oprah Winfrey or Bill Gates, Hillary Rodham Clinton or even our man Biden, they would obviously go and buy their clothes from such places like, Oscar de la Renta (the most expensive store in the USA based of course in New York, Madison Square Garden). Other celebrities wouldn't mind seeing their visitors (angels) wearing clothes from, Georgio Armani, Blake of Chicago, Maxfield, West Hollywood, LA, Bloomindales or even Cyberdog of London. Some high–end clothes from Paris, let us say, Lacoste would not be bad at all. These high-end types of clothing are out of reach for regulars, like you and me. Nevertheless, every angel can afford to get (or just take) any of these and from any store of their choice. It is not the problem of money; it is about what station in life of that person. Angels would dress up to suit the circumstances of their host. Angels do not lack silver or gold like Peter. Money is not an issue; remember, their Boss has more money than all billionaires combined do.

Money is not a constraint to angels. What is critical is figuring out how to blend in. Using the accepted style of their host is a challenge. I am sure by now you have figured out that angels do not discriminate when it comes to service (more on this later). If they were to visit the rich in the Middle East, they make sure they are dressed in attires that fit their class and occasion. Jewell is very popular in that place of our world. Since that is the case, angels likewise would wear jewels. They cannot make a mistake of appearing like beggars. It is fair to say that most people from the Middle East may prefer to shop at *Cartier (those who have the means)*. How do angels conduct themselves among the middle class? Do angels have to change what to wear when they visit middle class? The answer is a resounding, yes. So let us look where they will go to buy clothing they would need in order to visit people in middle class.

Angels and the middle class

The middle class trends are a bit tricky because some push themselves to look outstanding even though they cannot afford to shop on Fifth Avenue.

They tend to find a way to appear as though they have the money like the millionaires. They monitor where the rich donate their clothes and then shop there. Some go to outlets where certain particular brands of clothing are relatively cheap but it is the same version that the rich would buy. The middle class try to dress up that way in order to find a way to mingle with the stinking rich. Some rich people are very particular when it comes to appearance. They take note what people are wearing and can differentiate whether you are rich or a struggler. People go a long way to be accepted in society. Fashion outlets have become the salvation of middle class.

Middle class love to shop at less expensive stores like Mercy, Target, J C Penny, Abercrombie, Banana Republic, Nike, Nautica, Lancôme, Gap, Coach, Calvin Klein, H&M, Adidas, and much more. To elevate themselves to look like the rich kid next door, middle class prefer to buy stuff at discount outlets that carry popular brands. Angels are aware of these trends; therefore, they make sure they adorn themselves in these styles when they visit the middle class. They know what we love and do. Do not forget that when they visit they have a game plan. Their goal is to try to avoid any semblance of suspicion. They disguise themselves by any possible means when they pay a visit to any particular individual. They prefer to garner acceptance like any normal human being would. They do not just come at random at all. Their planning include their outfit and the appropriately language to use. That of course as we have said includes manners and customs of particular countries. They are better at observing traditions of people than the locals themselves. That is why we easily miss them when they are in our midst. We think we are just talking to the Johnnies, Maries, Hosea's, and Bob's in our community. If there are any sentient, who knows how to travel incognito angels are the best. They are just that good. You cannot outsmart them; they have more access to knowledge than all our minds put together! Just think how long it takes you to put together that outfit you are now proud of. Would you not appreciate if you met another person dressed just like you? Angels take all of these into considerations. In all this, you will appreciate that angels get dressed tailored to their audience. Angels do not attract attention to themselves. That is the point. They came to visit someone and they want to be comfortable with that individual. Everything angels do, is tailored to their hosts. In other words, whatever they come to accomplish, is about you. If their Boss sent them to you, they will dress like people in your neighborhood.

Angels outfit are tailored towards their hosts

If angels were to visit the White House or the nobility, they would be dressed like dignitaries probably in self- tailored clothing and shoes. Where would they get self-tailored clothing? Angels are very resourceful. They are able to use stuff that is already made and available but unused. They can easily obtain clothing, shoes, and other stuff because they are invisible and have easy access to a lot of things without being noticed. Their ability to camouflage so deceitfully has enabled them to speak or even eat with us on our own tables without realizing it. Have you been suspicion of a person in your life? Angels are very good at disguising themselves. It is very hard to distinguish them from ordinary human beings. If they go to China, for example, angels will look like Chinese and eat with chopsticks. If they are in India or Middle East, they will dress likewise and eat a lot of hot stuff. If they are in Mexico, angels will make sure to eat some beans. Angels are international dignitaries who could go anywhere at any time and be accepted instantly. They can be sent to any part of our planet without needing translators because they are affluent in all the languages of the world. They are the best ambassadors the world has ever seen. They represent heaven extremely well. Their Boss is very happy with the work they do. Let me stress the point one more time; clothing, language, and manners and customs are critical to the success angels. If they were to visit people while at a Super Bowl, they will be dressed like fellow fans with weird hairdo, messed up jeans, and doing other funny stuff. If they are watching basketball, baseball or soccer, they will participate exactly like any human would at such events. Angels are great imitators of anything and you will not even know it. Are you by now wondering whether angels can visit the poor or people who are struggling in life? The answer is a resounding, yes. Going by statistics, angels have visited lowly people more than the rich and famous. Their focus is not on status; whether you are rich or poor. I gave you three reasons above why an angel may visit you. It has nothing to do with fame. They look at human beings in general as a total package of lost souls. Every human being has value, whether rich or poor. Would angels dress differently when they meet people on the lower end of the spectrum? The answer is definitively, yes. Angels will dress up appropriately to the group they plan to visit, and appear just like them. I cited an example about Kenyan or Zambian poor. Their MO-is "appear like your host" in every way. Angels dress up accordingly so that anyone can feel comfortable in their midst. Famous people such as Mary, the mother of Jesus, Mother Teresa, or **Mahatma** Gandhi may find it easier to mingle with angels. What is amazing and intriguing is that once an angel meets a poor person, that person's status changes forever. Normally when an angel visits a rich person, they tend to help them change their purpose for the use of their wealth. Good angels always bring something positive to the people they visit (rich or poor). When angels have visited kings or rich people, it has always been to help them have a right attitude towards the oppressed. David was given a parable on how badly he behaved towards his servant. His heart brunt up and he ended up writing Psalm 51, a beautiful picture of what real repentance looks like. However, if the rich people fail to change, usually negative consequences tend to follow them. I will now address how they pay for the stuff.

How angels pay for things they use

Angels are capable to get clothes from any store at any time free. As anyone seen an angel paying for stuff they have? Let us remind ourselves that angels have the ability to enter any store without being noticed. We should never forget that. It would be an angel. Everything would be free (money, food, clothes, shoes--just become a spirit and enter the store or a bank and help yourself)? Imagine getting free stuff and that means no paying tax (a dream for billions of people). Can an angel get some free money from Uncle Sam's bank while he is sleeping? Can angels do this? Are angels stealing when they get designer clothes without telling the owners? What if they plan taking them back would that making it justified? We can return something we bought if we do not like it. Can angels do likewise? Of course, they could. Would angels rent stuff in the absence of the owner as long as they take it back? They could put money in the cashier's drawers so that when it is time for inventory it would balance. It looks like these personalities have more options than we do. Can their Boss allow them to take the stuff in the absence of the earthly owner? Would that constitute stealing? Alternatively, can their Boss allow them to go back and pay for the things later? Is it possible that they pay for clothes before wearing them? Their Boss claim to own all things that exists. How that could be considered stealing? Alternatively, do they have to get money somewhere (mouth of a fish) and then pay for the goods? Angels can also get money from their Boss to pay for their attires directly. If he sends them on a mission, he is responsible to make sure that they get what they need to accomplish their goal. We do not know how exactly it plays out. What we do know is that angels always come already prepared with all they need. It is also true that if they wear real human clothes, which they do, then something happened. Maybe in future an explanation will be given. What we also know is that whatever they use, it is temporary.

Angels use earthly stuff temporarily

It is fair that angels do not take the stuff they use back to heaven. The leave these stuff behind for earthly use. Either they find a way to return them where they got them, or they donate them. I also believe stealing is not part of their vocabulary. Whatever things they use rightly belongs to their Boss. Their Boss is the one who has authorizes what stuff to be used. Interestingly angels used the stuff for communicating with people in a normal way. Their Boss sends encouragement to people through angels. What he does is beneficial to people. In other words, the stuff is used for a noble purpose. *Call it greater good.* Somehow, when angels come to visit somebody, they take into account everything they need while on earth. Clothing is an essential part of that deal.

83

Angels then plan and think where to get the particular attire to help blend in. After work is accomplished, clothes, jewelry, shoes, hats, and belts are then donated, most likely to thrift stores (more on this later). We have heard that anything is possible with their Boss. That means there are many options available on how to dispose of the stuff when the mission is over. What makes sense the most to me is that, angels get clothes from any store and probably pay for them. They then put the money in the cashier's tills (their boss paid Temple tax by getting money from fish). The two scenarios above make sense. Clothes can be returned or donate to any Thrift Store.

So far, what we have discussed outfits angels buy in stores. However, angels have designer tailored outfit specifically for them. Their special clothing cannot be found in our stores. Angels rarely use this stuff. They prefer to use our brand. Let us call these special clothes by their real name, heavenly outfit. These clothes are worn to display the glory of their Boss. These may not necessarily be real clothes. They are ordinary clothes that can dazzle by using special effects. It is not up to angels to use flash dazzling clothes. Angels are disciplined entities who follow instructions to perfection. How disciplined are angels when they come below? The simple answer is that they extremely disciplined. They do not deviate from their mission. They neither subtract nor add anything. Besides, they are in collaboration with their Boss in seconds. They are Spirit beings just as their Boss is the perfect Spirit. I referred to angels as disciplined, let me make a few points here.

Angels are disciplined

If there is a class of personalities that is well disciplined, angels are on the class of their own. Unfortunately, that has not always been the case all the time. A few angels failed the test. The angels flanked the test were expelled from their original home. They became known as demons or evil angels (same name as fallen angels). From that time, the rest of angels who did not rebel became known as elect or holy angels. Notwithstanding, our interest is centered in discussing good angels (elect or holy). All elect angels have access to a whole range of stuff found on our planet. As we saw earlier, these personalities have access to all shopping Malls in the universe. There has been no report that angels were caught stealing something. Since angels are spirits, they can enter any Bank or store without being noticed. It would be easy for these angels to take stuff from stores and give them to the poor. If angels were to get stuff without authority from their Boss and give it to the poor, the number of poor people could drastically be reduced. However, it never happens because of their character. They follow orders from their Boss. Some of our children steal stuff and give it to other friends. Their boss claim to have made the world and everything in it and yet he has never sent angels at night to get stuff from the rich and give it to the poor. You agree with me that this is among the most puzzling thing in the whole world. Their Boss does not permit that and they abide by that rule. Even evil angels do not go to the bank, take money, and give it to the poor. If angels have access to shopping Malls and stores, including banks, it means they have access to everything.

Angels have witnessed people die of starvation and yet no one sees them scooping into a restaurant, get food, and give it to the poor. They do not enter any groceries at night in order to get groceries and give food to the poor. If their Boss were to decide, he could give them money to distribute to everyone on earth and end poverty over night! Angels know people who have stolen money from other people. They know where these thieves live. They can go there get the money back and either return it to the owner or give it to the poor. Remember that human sometimes take such actions, angels do not because of discipline. Yes, I agree with you, this is one of the most amazing problems to explain. Should angels help the poor? You can see that angels do not envy the rich nor despise the poor. They are nonaligned and disciplined. They strictly follow orders from their Boss. That is incredible! If the asset of invisibility were given to thieves, the idea of keeping money in banks would be counterproductive. There would be no money in banks. The idea of banks would never have existed. There will be no poor person on earth either. I would even say that the rich would not exist. Life would be predictable. What do you think? That is incredible. Yet we have personalities right now who are invisible but can also be visible. They do not misuse their invisibility because they follow orders all the time. They have the discipline of the highest caliber. Picture the difficulties thieves go through to steal. What if they were given the abilities to be invisible and get anything they needed? Would you like to be invisible and do what you want? What is going on in the spiritual world? Yet angels have easy access to anything in the world.

Angels have easy access to the stuff

Angels have easy access to anything in the world. Think about it, angels have access to all auto malls on earth and yet they do not take cars from Chicago and drop them in Zambia for the needy. If they were to transport vehicles, auto dealers would be in big trouble. These angels can transport stuff in thin air from one point to another in no time. A man called Phillip (Acts 8) was made to be instantly moved from one place to another without a plane or a car. Apostle Paul was caught up in third heaven without a rocket. Jesus went up into heaven without a rocket. That power is available before the Boss of angels. They can accomplish any feat that seem impossible to human eye. Why not use it to transport food from the rich to the poor and around the world. If we cannot take unauthorized food, why not give the food that is thrown away to the needy. Food is being thrown away every day and yet people are dying of hunger somewhere. Angels can be the agents who could carry out that exercise. You know as I do, they do not do that. They are admonished not to, and they do not do it because they are well disciplined. We are talking about entities that have tremendous privileges in creation and yet they hold themselves together and always please their Boss, no matter the insurmountable injustices they see in the world. They only do what they are told. They trust their Boss because they know what He is up to. I confess, I am puzzled but I am ignorant of His ways.

Imagine an angel has been sent to visit someone on earth. While in transit and before arriving at his destination, sees a woman in a village in some country in Zambia, Africa. The woman is pregnant, carrying a baby on her back, walking bare feet, holding firewood on her head,

Courtesy-internet

while holding another bag in another hand. The angel in transit knows that the person he is visiting owns many cars and they are just lying around unused. Yet the visiting angel on his way, who can transport anything instantly, does nothing to help a poor woman in Zambia who is overburdened! Should the angel sidetrack and lender help to the woman in need? An angel cannot do because they follow orders with precision. They carry out and deliver the message without deviation. You may have heard stories where a man had locked up a woman in a basement for many years and yet an angel may visit that city but would not free the woman if the visit were for a different purpose. If issues depend on what angel's desires, they would do what feels right. That is not the case. They follow orders. Their Boss knows every ugly thing going on under the heavens and He could order trillion of angels to correct any issue on earth instantly. They know that their Boss has rescued people before when he deemed it necessary. They trust their Boss because they believe He knows what he is doing. To be honest, I am perplexed but what do I know about life!

The scenarios cited above prove that angels are well-disciplined beings. Angels do not steal anything because they are disciplined. One of the reasons they do not take our stuff is that they do not need these things on a permanent basis. When they wear our outfits, it is for our sake. In addition, angels have their own brand of clothing. Let us very briefly examine their brand.

Special clothing for angels

No person on our planet knows who designs the shining clothes. Their special outfits are probably made by using special effects. They cannot be found in stores. Special clothing was meant to intimidate or impress their hosts. Only a few people in our world had a glimpse of these elegant outfits. Angelic clothes create a mark of distinction. They are in the class of their own. When angels appear wearing such clothes, it is usually to make a clear point to the person they are paying a visit. Unfortunately, no one has ever elaborated in details why they wear such remarkable stuff. Have you ever worn a shining dress or suit? I am asking you billionaires. You call that shining. You have never really seen what shining is until the day you will meet an angel dressed in such. The white pieces of linens they sometimes appear in are exceptional and heavenly, to say the least. The good book affirms that sometimes angels appear wearing shinning clothes. Look it up if you are in doubt in the books of Luke, Acts and Revelation (Luke 24:4; Acts 10:30; Rev. 15:6) respectively. The angels appeared like men (even our beloved millionaires and billionaires have no access to such angelic wardrobes -apologies). When some women met these angels in such attires, they were dazzled and terrified. Their clothes shone with intensity, brilliance and immensity in such way that it created terror in the women and a man (called John who lived on an island called Patmos). Shinning clothes was a mark of separation from their regular appearances.

Clothing that shine

When the Son of their Boss rose from the dead, a few angels appeared to people in shinning clothes at his graveyard. This may appear as fiction to some but to others who believed the story of the risen man it was a sign of new beginnings. There is another name that is used to define these clothing; it is called, "pure white (Acts 1)." Their Boss appeared in these kind of clothes only once in his life on earth (Matthew 17:1-4) before the resurrection. However, right now we are only interested in shining clothes –the special brand for angels. If you are an American or have lived in the USA for a long time, your mama should have introduced you to the book and you should know what we are talking about. Most movies depicting angels have taken a few lines from the good book. USA is one of the lands where the good book has been celebrated for a long time even though many do not seem to obey its contents.

There are more Bibles in the United States than there are in the entire continent of Africa (Africa has over a billion people)! Your mama expects you to know better. The shinning clothes reflect the character of their Boss because he decides what attire to use at any given time. It is extremely rare to see angels in shinning clothes. We know of one man and two women so far who saw them in shinning clothes. Mark this; angels have appeared in shinning clothes less than five times in the entire good book. That excludes pure white clothing, that believers will be dressed in some day. The good book tells us that angels have appeared about 100 times in the Old Testament and over 160 in the New Testament, and have worn ordinary human clothing most if not all the time.

Let me make final points before we consider where they donate or leave used stuff. I will do that by telling a Cinderella story. The best picture of how angels appear incognito is perhaps the Cinderella story you may have heard your father or mother read to you a long time ago. Let us quickly recap and get some similarities.

The Cinderella story

The story of angels mingling with people is likened to the story of Cinderella who appeared incognito before the prince. These magnificent great angelic creatures have appeared to the rich, the poor, and even to middle class like you and me. They appeared incognito just like Cinderella did before the rich Prince. The major point of comparison of Cinderella story is in the very last line, ("The word "<u>Cinderella</u>" has, by analogy, come to mean one whose attributes were *unrecognized*, or one who unexpectedly achieves recognition or success after a period of obscurity and neglect.)"

Here is the point; we cannot recognize the attributes of angels when they come. Nevertheless, we can tell the good things that follow after they pay a visit to someone. Cinderella had such element and won the heart of the Prince. She blended in at the special occasion. She did that to fit in. Just like angels do. Afterwards Cinderella had to dispose her special clothing and shoes afterwards. That is exactly what angels do. That is their game plan all the time. Angels do not carry these clothes to heaven and so where do they leave them.

Where Angels Drop used Stuff

There are no stores in heaven. Angels do not need earthly stuff up there. Where then do they leave the stuff they used? My sneaky suspicion suggests that they donate them. Surely, the best place to leave the stuff is none other than Thrift Stores across the world. It is not wise to leave clothes on the doorsteps of poor people. That might mean trouble for them. They may be accused of stealing (especially if things look new). Donating stuff used in Thrift Stores is the best way to go.

The MO they used to obtain the apparels is likely to be the same they will use to dispose them. In Zambia, used clothing is known as "salaula." Let me say something you least expected to hear; the best place to buy clothes is to buy used clothes (salaula). I know what you think especially if you are rich. You may argue that you will never buy anything from salaula. That is all right. Let me defend my reasons for suggesting that. I will give one point right now but more to come later. *Thrift Stores gives you the best chance to wear something worn by heavenly celebrities.* Think about that! Consider how we desire to use something a famous person had. We call some of the stuff antique. They are very expensive to buy them at auctions sales. Usually people with a lot of money are able to buy the stuff. Only Thrift Store gives the rich and the poor equal opportunity to buy something invaluable at a giveaway price. You may buy something extraordinary worn by a celestial being. It is your choice. Therefore, it is better to say never, in life. You never know what you may buy at salaula. I will write more on this later. I know that human beings are more proud than a white peacock. Humility wins the day. Even the good book as a lot to say about pride. My point, find your way to Thrift Store, you will unearth amazing blessings. That is where angels leave behind their used stuff. Angels do not need clothing or shoes in heaven. When they get back to heaven, they are transformed into their original state. There are no factories for clothing and shoes in the entire heaven. By extension, it also means that there are no places to store the stuff. Shopping stores such as, Hermes, Georgio Armani, Blake of Chicago, Maxfield, West Hollywood, LA, Bloomindales or even Cyberdog of London are never mentioned nor found in the heavenly places. Therefore, clothes, shoes, and any other materials will never find their way in the living quarters of angels. Clothes and shoes worn on earth are earthly and therefore belong to the earth. They are not needed in the invisible world. Put it crudely, spirits have no need of material stuff. Strugglers and poor people frequent Thrift Stores and that is where some get their blessing without realizing it. A word to the wise, do not go to Thrift Store in a rich neighborhood. If you would like to take a chance and buy, stuff left behind by angels, visit common middle class Thrift Stores. You say what? You may argue and say that it is not a place to find good stuff. Yes, that is true, but chances of finding stuff left by angels are good there. The rich tend to donate to a particular class of people, and the middle class run there. The Boss to angels knows that and therefore he makes sure that his angels donate to areas where such opportunities to have great stuff are rare. That is the best-kept secret.

The best kept secret

Angels generally donate to the very needy middle class thrifts in the neighborhood. It is one of the best-kept secrets in world affairs. Some very poor people may have won clothes worn by angels. What a touch of heaven! How would you like to wear a shirt worn by JFK, Abraham Lincoln, Obama, Michelle, Trump, Mandela, Oprah, Gandhi, Kamara Harris or a shirt worn by the President of the United States! Now compare these to having attire worn by visitors from Heaven! It is your choice. That is how amazing things work on our planet. Here is a deal. There is a way you can raise the chances of buying clothes won by angels. Here are a few points to help you achieve that goal. How to distinguish things used by angels and those that are ordinary.

First: New clothes but no tags

Have you ever bought some clothes at thrift stores with tags intact? This is one of the clues to look for. If the tags are not removed, it is a sign that they are not from angels. Earthly rich people do that. Angels are extremely smart. They remove tags right away. Besides, they do not buy stuff in bundles. Whatever they buy, it is for use that day. They do not visit someone wearing their clothes with tags unremoved. *They cannot come to your house with tags on; that would be shallow.* The rich people tend to buy so much such that they never even wear some of these clothes and eventually donate them to Goodwill or any other Thrift Stores. Remember angels return to heaven the same day. They never sleep on earth. Whatever they buy the use it for a couple of hours only. The rich if they kept the piece of clothing for too long and their stuff is out of fashion, they donate such with tags on. That is a very good sign that it is not from angels but rich people. I am not saying that all new clothes without tags are from angels. Many might be, but not all. However, all clothes with tags are never from angels. Watch out for new clothes without tags, socks, neckties, and shoes. You have the best chance to buy stuff used by angels in that way. The point is; any clothing or shoes that still have tags are not from angels. It is a good thing to buy new clothes; it is good for you but if you are trying to increase, the chances of buying clothes used by angels go to Thrift Stores and buy new stuff but without tags. That is the first sign. Remember, why you would like to buy such stuff; you are looking for an *heavenly touch*. Heavenly touch brings heavenly blessings and last a long time. The second sign is to buy clean clothes.

Second: Very clean clothes-but not washed

Very clean to brand new is the way to go. You have good chances to wear a piece of material or shoes and even socks worn by heavenly visitors. It is not a joke I am giving you excellent points you rarely find today. If you have, high opinion of the good book then take it from here that you have a better chance to wear angelic outfit. If you find something newer, clean or brand new altogether, consider buying it. Their clothes are clean because they come from a place where dust does not exist. Their bodies are absolutely clean. They will leave cleans clothes behind all the time. Angels have no time to take clothes to dry cleaning. Let us use some common sense. When they take stuff to Salvation Army, Good will and any other Thrift stores for that matter, they are never washed or dry-cleaned. Thrift Stores encourages us to donate washed or clean our clothing before we donate them. That is just common sense. If something appears to have been worn, in excellent condition, no sign of dry-cleaning or washed, angels may have donated them. If there are signs of being washed, or dry-cleaned, it is not a mark of angelic outfit. We can also look at it from a negative point. Let us state a few negative guiding signs. Second point is very similar to the first but with few valuations. If it appears clean due to dry cleaning or being washed, it is not from angels.

Third: Very old clothes are not from angels

Very old clothes are a sign that they are from middle class people or even the middle poor (call them working poor). Do not be deceived by brand names on clothing. Even clothes or shoes with brand names may come from middle poor or even poor people (watch the age not just the brand name). In the USA, there is a tradition of giving back. Some stuff with brand names could have been "recycled" several times. Brand name clothing and shoes find their way back to thrift stores many times because even the poor after having worn them feel good to give back to the stores things that seem to have value. Have you noticed that it does not matter how old these stuff may be? They are still expensive even in thrift stores. The catch is how old are these stuff. Look them over repeatedly. Angels may blend in among the poorest of the poor and use such attires! However, they never donate such stuff because they know morally that it is not helpful to give something that is almost worn out. They can dress in any attire even poorly in order to blend in, but such attire is not donated. If you buy clothes that are too old, you will never have a chance of wearing clothes worn by angels. Angels do not donate clothes that are too old. Very old or dirty clothes are negative signs that they were brought there by angels. Blessings only apply to the first purchaser and are not transferable. Angels can wear very old clothes but do no donate them. To wear what angels wore is one of the best-kept secrets. It is far better than wearing what the president of the United States wore! The three principles are able to guide you what to buy that gives you a better chance of using things used by angels. That then tells a wise person to shop from middle class Thrift Stores.

Shop from Thrift Stores

My family and I have been to Goodwill a couple of times. We have been to Salvation Army and other Thrifts Stores when times were challenging. We thrived using some recycled stuff. Things change my friends and we live in unpredictable world. One day you are rich, the next you are in rugs. If pride gets hold of you, you will die young. Humility is the greatest medicine for survival. We survived. Even a friend of mine who is now a millionaire shopped at these places of honor. He has since moved out. He is now thriving in luxury. Countless people once were poor and shopped at thrifts. Yet some people who were once rich are now visiting Thrift Stores. It is a good place to buy antique stuff whose price would be prohibitive if purchased brand new in regular stores. One of my daughters used to buy only certain items but not anything used for eating (I have three so; no one knows which one I am talking about). Whenever she sees something in the kitchen that she has never seen before, she would inquire, "is this new or where did you get it?" She was free to buy other stuff. While at Thrift Store, it is very interesting if not amusing to notice people hang around waiting for the new line of stuff to be displayed. That is wisdom because that is the time to grab the best piece. The best time to chance to get newer things is when the sales representative is just displaying them on the regular lines. As you would expect, shoppers scramble for them. I was walking on the streets of Lusaka and saw people scramble for things that were just being displayed. That happens everywhere, in USA all the way to Zambia. What is happening is that they are taking chances to get the best after the workers have picked theirs. That is another excellent opportunity that may land you into wearing a piece worn by heavenly hosts. It also reveals that volunteers and workers have the greatest opportunity to get angels' used stuff. Well, you are free to volunteer and keep your eyes peeled. Now you know how to identify what angels used. Do you now appreciate why angels do not disclose where they donate their worn clothes? No one could afford to buy them if the owners knew that angels wore them. They would be too expensive to sale. They may not even try to sale them. Which foolish person would dare do that? Angels are persons who live in the presence of the greatest power in the entire universe. It would be utter foolishness to sale the stuff that came from the hosts of heaven.

Angels do not take stuff to heaven

Let me state a helpful point; you will never have a chance of wearing angelic clothes if you buy brand new clothes or shoes directly from the stores. Angels do not return clothes to these stores at all. They also do not leave them on the doorsteps of poor people. Thrift Stores are the most sensible venue to drop used stuff. It creates an equal opportunity to different classes of people. When the poor buy them, they have the receipt to prove that they did not steal, if the stuff looks new. We must all remember that angels are constantly visiting people who are hospitable. Let us make something very clear here: Angel's sole purpose of their existence is ministry to people. It is true that they minister to their Boss, but he can do without them. We need angels more than God does. Angels are intermediaries. They do not just sit in heaven. Yet there are angels whose job is to bring a touch of heaven to people on earth, especially to those who are in the habit of hospitality. We must also remember that most humans are not hospitable and that is why visitation is rare. Real and heart felt hospitality will attract heaven. Heaven will bring blessings. Buying used clothes from angels will also bring some measure of blessings. Remember a woman who touched the garment of Jesus and were healed? Angels represent Jesus. Touching garment they wear will make a difference. The only bad news in all these attire is that you cannot buy their special clothing that shine.

People do not wear angel's shining stuff

We doubt if such shinning clothes worn by angels can be dropped in stores for resale. Such clothes may raise great suspicions. The majority of angels would like to come incognito and do not use shinning clothes at all. Some of course do. There is no way that such heavenly "gear" would be sold on earth. First, they would be too conspicuous and expensive to buy them. Maybe the billionaires and the queens or the King of England might. Even for the richest people, they would be too expensive to afford. Furthermore, they would attract untold number of people and the glare would be too much to endure. There is zero chance that any human being would have a chance to use them anyway. These attires were meant for angels only. They were meant for very special occasions. My sense is that, they are ordinary clothes that are made somewhere unknown. I do not see why angels who are spirits carry these clothes in heaven. We should also remember that the clothing that shines might be ordinary, but angels may use "special effects" just like movie actors sometimes employ such methods to dazzle us. For example, the appearing of a few people on the mountain was pure use of special effects because it did not last long. Nevertheless, it created an impact on those who witnessed it. Likewise, the dazzling white linen by angels is very short lived. Their Boss could illuminate such with a special touch.

Best shopping stores

For goodness sake, buying clothes in thrifts is the best way to go for anyone who would like to wear heavenly gear. Life is funny, the poor the rich look down on, are the very ones who tend to praise them! Interestingly, no one forbids rich people from shopping at salaula market places, only their pride hinders them. Thrifts stores are places of equal opportunity for anybody. These recycled goods are the second best means in getting indirect contact with angels other than hospitality. As you now know, the best opportunity to touch angels is hospitality to strangers. Taking chances at thrifts has nothing to do with hospitality. Hospitality stands alone as a virtue recognized by greater powers. Hospitality gives the greatest opportunity to anyone to encounter a real angel compared to any other methods. As I have pointed out, there have been remarkable changes by men and women who came in personal contact with angels. Their lives were changed forever. I have a sneak suspicion that all the best minds and more so the so-called geniuses, the likes of Einstein might have had indirect angelic contact without knowing it (I have no evidence on this). It is possible that these geniuses will have rubbed shoulders indirectly with heavenly visitors who may have shaped and helped change the course of the world. Remember, no genius ever created his or her own mind. So either they were gifted at birth, or they had an angelic encounter indirectly. We have shown how some lives have been changed after interacting with angels. Something happened to these geniuses also in the process of time. From the biblical point of view we have noticed that any person who were exposed to angels have had their lives changed. Those changes have affected millions of people worldwide. It is not overstretching to say that we might not know with certainty the paths these geniuses may have passed through which made them "change" the world (did they buy used clothes unknowingly). At the minimum, these humans may have touched something angels touched.

PART 4

Other Important Facts about Angels

Do not under estimate the power of angelic touch-No human being ever created their own mind so as to make themselves genius. A genius does not create his/her own mind we should remember that. Abraham did not make himself great. Jacob did not change his own name by sheer changing the constituent of his mind. So do not under estimate the idea of coming in touch with angels. These contacts have huge implications in human affairs. That is why entertaining a stranger is a very good thing to do. Why would we be advised to entertain strangers if there is no value in doing so? As far as clothing is concerned, even people who live in the third world countries have equal chance of buying and dressing in clothes worn by angels. That indeed always brings good things in life. No one will ever know except that some may get a blessing for wearing stuff used by heavenly visitors. Good angels always bring good news all the time. As of now, we advise that if you have any common sense, start visiting and shopping at these thrift stores mentioned above. At the same time, learn to be smart as you shop by adhering to the guidelines I have pointed. Look for newer unwashed clothing or at best something that does not appear to have been worn many times. Buy something without a tag but in great shape. You will never know what you bought; an angel could have worn it. However, when you start seeing that your fortunes are changing from worse to the best, consider the thought. Are angels broke of homeless? The brief answer is angels are neither broke nor homeless.

Angels are neither stranded nor homeless

Just because we are encouraged to entertain angels does not mean they are homeless or stranded. They are not, infact, they have a beautiful home called heaven. They come to the earth with a clear mission. They usually come to reward hospital people. They pretend to be strangers so that people are genuinely caring and hospitable. Those who do, reap generous rewards. Angels travel incognito on purpose so that they are not treated differently. They tend to hide their identity because they know that if they announced their title they would be well received. Bear in mind that they do not come to you because they missed bread and butter or some great wine. Their visit is for one reason alone; to let to you know that their Boss has recognized your hospitality. The implication of that statement is that if you continue in your hospitable mindset, you are likely to receive a rich reward. In other words, every day we carry on our business, someone is observing us not so much of what we say but what we do. In fact it is what we do to people we do not know. As you keep practicing hospitality to strangers, the next person you will be entertaining might be an angel! That means their Boss has been watching what you do. No one could fake his or her way to God. God will not let us know advance that he is sending his angels. If he did, it would make people pretend to be hospitable. That is what we do to our bishops and political leaders. We cannot hide the truth to Him who knows the secrets of our hearts. We are by nature very selfish people than caring. It takes guts and true love to have genuine hospitable spirit. Even billionaires, who have so much, tend to relate well to others in their circle than strangers.

Bear in mind, rewards are not always measured in monitory terms but the quality of life that one might be granted (you may be taken to paradise). Having a lot of money is not always a sign that blessings originated from heaven. Some people may win a jackpot. Some people are good at embezzlement. Other people worked hard for it. Some may have come from Ponzi schemes. Some may get it as inheritance and yet some is due to their hospitality. No one truly knows except those who have it and how they got it. However, the good quality of life with or without money is always a blessing from the Boss of angels. Hospitality is one definite means by which God can bless you. Rich or poor, either way, you will be rewarded according to your deeds. Desist envying the rich or vying to live their lifestyle. Be hospitable to strangers and the Boss of angels may cast His eyes on you. As you rub shoulders with angels when they come to you, is there a possibility of smooching? Is there evidence to suggest that these angels at some point smooched some people? We will find out later that question. I give you scenarios of how involved we are with angels. All the preparations of angels getting proper outfit, suggest that they are in our midst perform many human activities. Would that include emotional activities as well? Is it possible to have been kissed by an angel without knowing it? Think about this; angels come down and participate in everything that people do. What would stop them from participating in emotional affairs? They eat our food. They partake in drinking. They wear our jewelry, shoes, hats, watches, and wear clothes. All the arguments above prove to us that angels are heavily involved in human affairs. Where do they stop?

We know that angels make sure they dress appropriately before they meet their hosts. They know exactly where they intend to go. They know the person's character in advance; and they are not going there by accident. Well, the next thing we know is that they at premises of their intended host. They know we do not know that. That is where things gets trick. At the end of their visit, they have to follow the traditions of their host. What kind of greetings do they practice? Americans love to hug. Middle Easterners love to kiss. Others just shake hands like Zambians. Kissing in certain cultures is normal human expression, smooching is different. Kissing therefore mean different things in different among people groups. We have heard lyrics have expressed kissing an angel. What kind of kissing is that? Since Westerners sang it, we will take it in two meanings. Kissing kids is an expression of general love. Kissing an adult might mean something else. So then what do lyrics imply? Most likely kissing their girl friend or wife. When I explore do angels smooch, I am asking a general question that could that go either way.

First, it seems to me that we have never paid attention to the words in these expressions. We have heard so many lyrics or even watched movies portraying angels in a certain way. It is always in a positive light. Kissing is not a bad word at all. Their Boss namely Jesus was kissed on his feet (Luke 7:38, 45) by a woman and he did not stop her. Jesus challenged his host that he was not given a kiss but the sinful woman did. Yes, we know from biblical perspective that it was a traditional way of appreciating somebody. This is referred to as a holy kiss. Are angels excluded from a holy kiss? What would happen if angels were kissed? Let me be precise, did some angels kiss women in Genesis 6? Were the angels holy when they smooched women and then became evil after the act? Let us revisit the teaching on entertaining angels. We shall focus entertaining strangers who might be real angels. If people can entertain angels, then that is personal. The word entertainment is defined as, "the action of receiving a guest or guests and providing them with food and drink." That is exactly what Abraham did. What is the synonym of entertainment? Here we have it from the English language that include: "amusement · pleasure · leisure · relaxation · fun · enjoyment · interest · occupation · refreshment · restoration · distraction · diversion · divertissement and many more. If all these words are possible meaning of the word entertainment then our question is valid; can they kiss? Can angels smooch as part of entertainment? To answer that question, we need to revisit some arguments we have looked at before.

Revisiting People who Encountered Angels

We have alluded to the idea of entertaining before. We shall now dig further and unearth what we do not know yet. Talking about entertaining angels, there are a lot of references in the Bible itself. One of the most famous stories that leave no doubt in our minds is the narrative in Genesis 18. We read that Sarah and her husband took time to prepare a meal for the three visitors. Abraham had no clue that they were angels. We know that now because the narrator has told us but Abraham did not know. The visitors clearly ate the food set before them. Here is a brief recount of that narrative. We begin reading from verse 4 of chapter 18, "Abraham said, if I have found favor in your eyes, my lord, do not pass your servant by.[4] Let a little water be brought, and then you may all wash your feet and rest under this tree.[5] Let me get you something to eat, so you can be refreshed and then go on your way—now that you have come to your servant. "Very well," they answered, "do as you say."[6] So Abraham hurried into the tent to Sarah. "Quick," he said, "get three seahs of the finest flour and knead it and bake some bread."[7] Then he ran to the herd and selected a choice, tender calf and gave it to a servant, who hurried to prepare it.[8] He then brought some curds and milk and the calf that had been prepared, and set these before them. While they ate, he stood near them under a tree. End of quote. Notice that these were total strangers to Abraham. He had never met them before.

The visitors agreed to all that Abraham suggested, including washing the feet. These men had sandals on them. Abraham was able to see their feet and toes. They were nothing but real humans. They rested under a tree as Abraham watched them eat meat and bread (solid food that needs digestion and excretion). It appears that one among the visitors was more than a mere angel. For now, let us set that aside. The three of them appeared as males and had a clear mission they wanted to accomplish. If these visitors ate meat, then they had teeth to bite and chew it. They did not eat meat they came with. In fact, from what we read, they were not carrying anything with them. They ate meat and drunk something set before them. They were human by all accounts. They did everything human do. Get this; *the way these visitors appeared to Abraham is exactly the same way they would appear to anyone in appropriate outfit.* Washing feet in those days was equivalent to taking a shower, and they did. Abraham did not say these feet look abnormal and they are not human. They had five toes and they looked like his feet. When we swallow food, we begin with ingestion followed by digestion after that excretion. Like ingestion, excretion has a couple of outlets to dispose the waste in our bodies. Disposing what is in our bodies involve a lot of outlets, poles, mouth, nose, anus, penus and others. Whatever these men ate and drank was disposed using normal human organs. These three men possessed all these organs. They drunk and therefore they had the means to excrete in a normal way. Let us not create our own preference when we come to some difficult Scriptures passages. We should not try to spiritualize things to suit our theology. The narrator presented the visitors as normal males carrying out activities that normal people do. They were real people and there was no pretense about that. When we try to explain Genesis chapter 6, we should not change the facts to suit our theology. God is not afraid to reveal anything at all. We should let the context and attributes of God help us understand a truth in any given Scripture. We should not come to a paragraph of Scripture and explain it using our particular theology. Having said that, let us continue examining the account in Genesis 18.

Angels' MO unchanged

Abraham did not know that these were angels. He had no idea that they came from heaven. That is why he respected them by merely addressing the leader as lord (small l). Abraham himself at times was addressed as lord (small l). He even followed the custom of the day of giving them water to wash their feet. He would not have done so if he knew they were from heaven. As far as he knew, he was talking to people like himself except that they were strangers to him. People on a journey needed food because there were no fast food restaurants (the Wendy's, Chipotle, McDonalds, Burger King and much more) in those days. The visitors must have stayed there a long time to wait for the food to be prepared. They were to bake bread on fire hood (no electricity and therefore no microwave ovens). They were to cook meat that takes some time to be ready. In the meantime, they should have been chatting while waiting for food to be ready. When everything was ready, visitors were then invited to eat. Culturally, eating in those days was an important cycle of events. They took their time chatting about all sorts of issues. They did not seem to be in a hurry either. Furthermore, one of them had a long discussion with Abraham when the other two had left. That is the longest discussion I have ever read involving a man and an angel. It took almost the whole day. Sarah had to cook real meat. It was not processed meat. Organic meat takes longer to be cook. Organic stuff took a couple of hours to be cooked. They used clay pots that do not conduct heat as good as metal. That slowed things further. They stayed in human form all that time. Since water and milk was also given to them, they may have been drinking it as they waited for meat to be ready. Bear in mind, these are spirits in human form talking to a mere mortal. Abraham welcomed strangers in his house without expecting anything in return. He was genuinely very hospitable person himself. No one told him that angels would visit him. Whenever good angel/s visits somebody, good things are likely to follow. If angels were to appear with wings and flying, everybody would welcome them with a smile. Few doubted the message of angels; for example, Zechariah (Luke 1:11) and Balaam are among a few people rebuked for doubting the message brought by angels. May be we can forgive Balaam because he could not actually see the angel but Zachariah should have known better. Zachariah thought the person talking was just a regular person. Gabriel had to make it clear that he stood in the presence of God (Luke 1:19). Instead of being commended, he received a rebuke, lost his sight, only to recover it after his son was born. Fortunately, his wife received the blessings. She got pregnant and bore him a son. We have referenced Mary, one of the famous stories in biblical history. Mary was not shocked for talking to a man because there was nothing special about his appearance. God sent his angel Gabriel to deliver a message to Mary (Luke 1:24). As far as Mary was concerned, the person standing next to her was just a man and not an angel. We know because the narrator has told us it was an angel. The appearance of angels without wings in human form is one of the fascinating stories in the Bible. Real angels do not have wings. For that matter, they do not need wings because spirits do not fly. Angels appears and disappears in flashes. Only in visions, trances, and dreams are angels depicted to have wings. I will explain that point later. However, keep in mind; angels have no use for wings. They are not material entities to possess material objects such as wings. When a person sees them in a trance or vision, they appear to have wings so that the person in a trance can see in the spirit realm. How can a natural eye see in the invisible world of spirits? That is only possible when God communicates to people using attributes of birds, animals or people in order to covey a truth. Wings speak of flight. That is why in visions we see angels flying. We cannot see angels flying with naked eyes. God can create that understanding by attributing these physical characteristics. God who is Spirit sometimes is depicted having, birds, animals and human characteristics but he does not possess any of these. That is the same thing with angels. No human being in natural state as ever has seen an angel with wings. They always appear without wings.

Angels in human bodies

One of the best-kept secrets in the universe is that angels are all around us. The depiction of angels having wings has misled many to believe otherwise. If you have read the Bible very well, no angel has ever spoken to a person with wings on their back. Every Scripture that references angels with wings is always captured through trances, dreams, and visions. In the actual world, since the creation of the world, at no time had an angel talked to a person and they said they saw wings on the back of angels. People by now would have taken pictures of real angels with wings. There is no prophet in the whole Bible who has seen an angel flying using normal eyes. Philip can tell you that. An angel came to him from nowhere and then just vanished. Birds that fly but angels do not do that. Why have angels never been seen flying with wings by Bible writers? God does withhold anything he would like us to know. He speaks his mind all the time. I will write more about wings later on. From the biblical accounts, we know that angels have the potentiality of immediate transformation from one state of being to another. That is to say, from spiritual, to material. God created them intentionally like so that they could mix with people. If the angels were to appear the way Hollywood depicts them, they would cause huge commotion. Furthermore, many would have pretended to be hospitable. Their Boss created them on purpose like that. As one can surmise, the rich as well as the poor have equal chance to receive a visit from an angel. God determines where to send an angel.

When Son to the Boss of angels came, he appeared as an ordinary person as he walked with two men on the road to Emmaus. At that time according to the good book, the angel's Boss had just risen from the grave. Jesus was in his glorified body but veiled to the eyes of these travelers; that is exactly how angels manifest themselves. Their Boss made them in such a way that they could take on human form. Use any human stuff. Speak a local language in any country. Be able deliver a message in a normal way, to any person. That is the best power of angels. Angels come incognito and we can never figure out unless they personally disclose themselves. Angels normally do not reveal themselves and if they did, it is very rare. We should remember that angels do not sleep in our homes. If someone slept in your home, it is a good sign he was not angels.

Angels do not stay overnight

I have so many best secretes to share with you: Another best-kept secret is that angels never sleep over. That helps you to distinguish fake and real angels. If someone sleeps over at your house then know with certainty that it was not an angel from above. That means you need to pay attention to strangers who pass by your home for a few minutes or a couple of hours. That is an important pointer to the truth! Could angels appear in the form of people of color? Angels are not prejudiced. Furthermore, they do not possess any pigmentation. Spirits do not have color bars. They appear in human form and therefore can appear as blacks, browns, whites, yellow and so on.

Are angels prejudiced (Hagar)?

Angels will look like a white, black, yellow person. Did you get that? Yes, angels will look like black, yellow person appropriately. Some will appear short or tall (*remember they have no skin color-they are spirits who have the ability to put on human form of that given ethnicity they are visiting*). They can appear in any skin color we found on earth. If that were not so, then angels will only appear to people who hold their skin color. The problem is that angels are ministering spirits and do not possess natural human form on permanent basis. They adopt human form when they are sent to people. That makes it easy for them to flow well in the lives of human beings. There you have it. Angels are sentient beings from a different planet with a powerful mission to a particular group of people. Everyone person has a chance to meet with the heavenly visitors. Racism was coined by the devil to promote evil. Racism or prejudices exist among people who sin. Holy angels do not even mention that. Spirits have no color bar. Any people who claim allegiance to God and practices racism, tribalism and caste system is an insult to God. It is like saying God is a sinner. Let us consider a few more insights regarding the attitude of angels towards people on the lower end of the spectrum.

How angels treaty people at the lower end of the spectrum

Unlike what the rich and famous do, angels are a different "breed" of creatures. They are sent to visit any person whether they are rich, famous (no one has monopoly on angelic visitation) or poor. The middle class, people at the lower end of the spectrum, and even the ignoble, all stand an equal chance to be visited by an angel. Most of us have heard of a story of a very poor man who survived by eating the crumbs falling from the table of a rich man. When both died, an angel took the poor man to Abraham's bosom. The angel did not base it on the status of the rich man as a criterion for such action to shame the rich. It was based on their attitude while living here on earth. (Remember we saw how an angel commended a wealth man because of his attitude - noble Cornelius). While on earth the rich always gets the best in terms of material stuff. However, do not misinterpret the story the wrong way. When an angel took the body of poor man Lazarus when he died, He did so based on the life he lived not his status. No one should imply that the rich could never be taken up in that manner. Judgment is based on how you lived your life on earth. Money is not the determinant. The point is this; the poor as well as the rich could be visited by heavenly hosts based on good life style. To think that angels cannot visit the rich and famous is a misrepresentation of the work of angels. They go by command from their Boss. Bear in mind that angels do not draw attention to themselves but point to their Boss. They are just mere messengers that come incognito to deliver the messages to some blessed individuals. The injunction reads, "Do not forget to show hospitality to strangers, for by so doing some people have shown hospitality to angels without knowing it." Did you notice the wording or the structure of the statement? It is not a onetime thing. It is not just in the past, but a continuous activity. It is not one person who may have worn the jackpot to entertain an angel. Some (many) people have entertained angels (many angels and many people). Notice the structure of the statement again; "Do not forget to show hospitality to strangers," present continuous and strangers are plural. Notice the statement is plural, angels' (many). There are many angels roaming around the world as we speak. Take heed and be wise, be hospitable to people especially strangers.

People have entertained angels

Many people have entertained angels in the past. There is a good chance that you too may entertain an angel. The question we need to ask is, why encourage people to have that attitude if there is nothing to be gained? On the contrary, there is much to be gained if you are hospitable. That good behavior has a payoff. On one thing is certain, you have helped someone who was stranded. On another hand, you too one day might be helped. That last stranger you helped may turn out to be an angel. Angels carry blessings with them. The point is that we still interact with strangers and some of these strangers may be angels who may bring benefits to you. No wonder Charlie Pride sung, "Kiss an angel good morning." You never know, it may be that last time a particular stranger who passed by your house was an angel. In biblical times, they used to greet one another with a holy kiss. You see that. Could that have involved angels too? What if your visitor was an angel and in the morning by way of greeting them, you gave them a holy kiss? Is there a possibility that such a thing has happened? It was meant to be a holy kiss and you took that visitor as a mere human being but you may have kissed an angel with a holy kiss. That is different from smooching! They did not smooch but kissed them as a way of greeting each other. Now if these visitors appeared and looked like humans, they too received a holy kiss as a form of greeting. Would you rather take the chance of meeting an angel or miss it because you inhospitable? If you are a racist, it is impossible to receive heavenly visit. You may have earthly blessings but have no heavenly touch. Earthly blessings are no sign that you are a good person even if you call yourself a Christian. Many people who are pagans today are rich. Many people who are Christians today are rich. Wealth is not a measure of heavenly touch. Are all rich people true followers of Jesus? You know that is not true. Equally true is that poverty is no sign that you are a true believer. There must be something to it? The truth lies in what is in your heart. You know the truth whether you are prejudiced or not. Many people are not hospitable. Many Christians who are prejudiced have no chance of being visited by an angel. Having a religious title is not a qualification of true follower of Jesus. A few true believers are hospitable. You can call yourself a Christian and live a life that is worse than a pagan is. The choice is yours. To reinforce the benefits of hospitality, let me give you the opposite of that. What would happen if you are inhospitable? Do we ever reflect about our behavior in life?

If you are inhospitable, you lose

If you are not a hospitable, chances of entertaining an angel are slim to none. People, who are prejudiced, are unlikely to be visited by an angel. Many in our world who look down on the poor will miss the best opportunity of entertaining angels. Here is another point why angelic interactions should be sought. *Angels may report your inhospitable attitude to their Boss in heaven.* Some claim to be Christians but their practices leave much to be desired. Some Christians are worse than non-believers. Just like some Jews were worse than Gentiles. Very few Christians seem to care for people who do not look like them. Merely having a label "evangelical Christian," does not automatically translate to be a good person. It is a well-established fact that no human being chose to be born in any given family, except Jesus. Jesus could have chosen to be born white or black, but he chose the middle ground; he was neither white nor black. The rest of us had no choice. To be punished for something someone never chose, is the worst kind of evil. Furthermore, it would be embarrassing to learn that the Latino you discriminated against was actually an angel who was sent to visit you. You may have had an opportunity to show hospitality but you blew it because of prejudice. You missed that great opportunity to entertain strangers because of something very silly, the color of their skin. Their Boss has kept the secret of sending angels in human form so that hypocrites will never have a chance to entertain angels.

Many people prefer to entertain people who belong to their class or who look like them. You are free to do that but you will miss a chance to entertain an angel. Remember, it has to be strangers. Anybody can be hospitable to people they like. In any case every so called a believer was at some point a non-believer. God created whites, Asians, Blacks, Latinos, Indians and so forth. You boast of being a religious person but you lack hospitality to strangers. Religious people get lost in their manmade theologies. Here are a few examples of popular religions that discriminate, Moslems, Judaism, Christianity, Hinduism, Shinto, to name but a few. Angels and their Boss do not belong to any religion in the world. His Son Jesus never created Christianity. His Son created the church. He told his disciples to make disciples not Christians (Matthew 28). His Father never created Judaism. He created a new nation called Israel. To be clear Jesus is not synonymous to Christianity. Neither is discipleship means Christianity. People in Antioch created the term Christianity. It was neither God, nor Jesus or his apostles; but gentiles in Antioch came up with that term, not Jesus. The Bible makes that very clear. We should also make it very clear that wealth or having modern technology is not a sign that their Boss is on your side. Their Boss does not endorse any political party. He does not and will never belong to any party, no matter what people may insinuate. The second point is that if you are inhospitable you may miss special protection. God sent an angel to protect Peter and Paul while in jail.

Do not miss special protection

The Boss of angels is very gracious to all his creatures. However, there are individuals who receive special favors. Included in that group are those who are hospitable. There are times when individuals are in dire need. You long for help immediately. Some good person sees you and without asking who you are, helps you out. That is what we talking about. It pays to be hospitable then and right now. The Boss of angels knows the contents of your character. He knows why you behave that way. When you disclose to your fellow rich person the favors you did to stranger, you have a motive right there. The context of hospitality is helping people in need, in trouble and abandoned without boasting about it. It is a big lie to say that all poor people are lazy or lack planning. Just because you hold that belief within your circles does not make it true. It may be true to some but not all. It is also not true that all rich people are stingy. Just accept that you do not like people. The poor will always be there, Jesus said and he does not lie. God never gave the poor the labels we have given them (lazy, poor planning). Why does God commend those who help the poor? Does God encourage laziness? That is why God told Israelites not to harvest everything but to live some for strangers and the poor. Well the question is does your hospitality measure up? Cornelius a gentile was commended for giving the gifts to the poor. They are genuine poor people. There are also poor people who are lazy. You cannot really know who is genuinely poor or lazy. Practice hospitality to strangers. There is yet another point the Boss's Son pointed out that come closer to entertaining angels. He said whatever you did to these least of brothers/sisters you did it to him (Matthew 25:45). Who are the least of brothers? Any person in need. If you help such needy people, angels might *report your name to their Boss*. Your name may come up one day and angels will give a report card to their Boss. They will recount how gracious and loving you were to other people. The number one goal of angels is to deliver a positive message to their Boss. That includes a report card about a nation or an individual. It is not what you say, but do your actions, move God. Unfortunately, none of us can manipulate God. Just be yourself. My suggestion to all of us is that it is time to begin practicing hospitality to strangers. Let us emulate people like Cornelius, Abraham and Tabitha. Your parents, your affluence, your money do not affect God favoring you, hospitality does. The most important point to remember is; what is in your heart.

It is how you treat others and especially strangers, affords you an opportunity to receive a visit from an angel. Angels can be in your house for less than a day. Angels may be strangers but they are not homeless as we said. They can pose as though they are lost on purpose so that a person with a genuine desire to help others might be revealed. Let me emphasis that point again, angels come to minister and not to receive help. They are not supposed to be worshipped. The white woman we helped was not an angel. She was a mere human being even though no one introduced her to us. We know that because she stayed longer than a day. Angels do not need buildings for shelter; they have beautiful spiritual homes high above us. All that is to say, angels interact with us on a daily basis but very briefly. However, the most important point to remember is that you are likely to be visited by an angel if you are a hospitable person. That stranger will then report your name to their Boss.

The other point not to miss is that angels are around us. They are watching us. They report us to their Boss. They may visit you in a form of a stranger. However, you might miss the opportunity to serve visitors from heaven because of inhospitality. You may miss special personal information regarding your status. Remember, angels will never tell you that they are from heaven so that you can act naturally. They may come as poor white man or poor black man. You will not know. Your heart will reveal itself what you are made of. If you are inhospitable, you will miss a blessings. However, remember, your negative report will still be sent to their God. My advice, treat every human as if they were all angels.

Angel may leave a souvenir

You never know, angels may leave clothes for you when they are gone from your home as a souvenir even if you did not know that they were angels! Have you wondered why you love that particular outfit? Do you really know-impressions, mere impressions-may be it is from an angel you entertained without knowing it. Do you know where they bought that shirt or dress they left you? May be from those very expensive shops where you can never ever afford one. You were left with high quality stuff because you gave that stranger some lunch and a place to rest. They were not really stranded; they came for a purpose to your house to test your claims. Either you passed or you failed the test.

Angels are ministering spirits

Let me remind you again that angels do not come to be entertained, they come to minister. They are called ministering spirits. It is they as their nature implies, who come to minister to you. That stranger you may have entertained could have come to render help to you. They have done that countless times. They have other reasons why they come to visit some people. In the book of Hebrews we are told "Are not all angels ministering spirits sent to serve those who will inherit salvation (Hebrews 1:14)?" They come to affirm your salvation. Can you put value on that? Friends, listen and examine these things.

Their Boss created them for one grand purpose, to be ministers. When they come to you, it is always about a payback. They are not there for your birthday cake to eat it; they are there to give you a better birthday gift. Sometimes they come to give you instructions on what to do as they did to Hagar. Other times they just want to let you know that you have received favor even if you did not earn it like Mary the mother of Jesus. Sometimes they come to help someone win a fight the way they helped Daniel.

In all these instances, they do not necessarily need what you gave them. They do not need anything from you. They came to minister to you. Would you for one moment think that angels who visited Abraham were going to die of hunger? Did they really need anything from Abraham or anybody to supply to their needs? Absolutely not! They always bring something amazing to hospitable and loving people. You lose nothing by helping strangers and you may end up helping yourself.

Elect angels do not need anything

Holy angels do not need anything from people. They do not need to know where to sleep shop or eat the food. They visit us for our sake. When they wear clothes, it is for our sake. When they visit homes, it is to bring a blessing. If you do not understand why we are encouraged to entertain strangers then you have missed the most important lesson why angels exist. They were created to mister not be ministered to. Even Satan was created to minister to God and to us, but he rebelled. Satan did not like the idea that he should minister to His Boss let alone people. He flipped that decree of God and demanded worship for himself. He was too proud to do that because his beauty. He wanted to be served rather than serve! Humans were not created to minister they were created to worship. Only angels were created to minister and worship. The only best thing we can do in this life is worship the angel's Boss. The rest of the things in the universe were given to us for our enjoyment. The Boss to angel does not need anything on our planet not even in heaven. All created things were meant for the enjoyment of the human beings and the glory for the

Creator who created all things. Their Boss does not need mountains, rivers, flowers, rain, sun moon or anything else. It is people who needs all the above. All we need to do is thank him and worship him. That is all that God desires from us. Just give thanks with a pure heart. God does not need anything that we see and do not see in the universe; he is self-sufficient. Can you imagine that angels were created to serve us. We give nothing back to angels. They are intermediaries who serve God and us. At least we worship God but we give nothing to angels. Have you pondered that? When they come to any person, they are not expecting anything for themselves from you. They came to serve you if are hospitable. Angels helps you even in fights.

Elect angels are your allies

Now follow this; as long as evil angels exists; we need good angels to help us. Holy angels and demons are able to see each other. They know who is in serious trouble and their Boss may decide to send an angel to minister to that person. Priority is always given to hospitable people. We read about the activities of angels; they do not build houses, they do not build airplanes, they are forbidden to get married. All that we read about them is either praising their Boss or helping human beings. Human beings are the only imitators of God. What do I mean? Humans participate in the role of creativity that God did. Angels are only preoccupied with serving not creativity. They do not need our stuff (water, land, mountains, etc.). All we read about is that they come to assist people like Hagar, Abraham, Daniel, Peter and many others in their times of need. The statement that states, you may entertain strangers, is a positive encouragement. It should not be taken as a burden but something to build you up. It is for our own good. We need to help each other and we shall receive help. Initially, the context of the given Scripture was directed to encourage Jewish believers. However, it is an open invitation to anyone. Let us now look closely at the work, and rank of angels. To appreciate the discussion, let me break down four divisions that exist in the universe. Below are the structures of powers that be.

PART 5

Brief Organization of Angels

A. The Godhead

    1. Rankings

        a. The Father

        b. The Son

        c. The Holy Spirit

B. Elect Angels

    1. Rankings

        a. Rulers,

        b. Authorities,

        c. Powers

        d. Spiritual forces

        e. Others

C. Fallen Angels

    1. Rankings

        a. Rulers,

        b. Authorities,

        c. Powers

        d. Spiritual forces

        e. Others

D. Human Race

1. Rankings

    a. President
    b. Senators
    c. Representatives
    d. Governors
    e. Rulers
    f. Others

I will not bore you discussing the rankings of Godhead or humans. I will focus on good angels.

Satan and evil angels work very well together. Because of that, many believe that Satan is everywhere. Satan appreciates that mindset because it makes him feel omnipresent, like God. Satan is only in one place at any given time. The structure of the organization of angels in found in the book of Ephesians, that says, "For our struggle is not against flesh and blood, but against the rulers, against the authorities, against the powers of this dark world and against the spiritual forces of evil in the heavenly realms (Ephesians 6:12-20)."

Rulers

"The rulers. . . . In the heavenly realms (Eph. 3:10; Eph. 6:12; Col. 1:6," this is referring to spirits or demons and Satan as those who rule in the invisible world, "heavenly realm."

Authorities

"His intent was that now, through the church . . . should be made known to the rulers and **authorities** in the heavenly realms (Eph. 3:10; Col. 1:16;

2:15)." Who has gone into heaven . . . with angels, **authorities** and powers in submission to him (1 Peter 3:22)," good angels is intended in this verse.

Powers

"In that day the Lord will punish the **powers** in the heavens above and the kings on the earth below (Daniel 4:35)." Powers here refers to evil angels. "He does as he pleases with the **powers** of heaven and the peoples of the earth. No one can hold back his or her hand or say to him, "What have you done? (Matthew 13:54)." Another reading says, "For I am convinced that neither death nor life, neither angels nor demons, neither the present nor the future, nor any **powers** (Romans 8:38),." "And having disarmed the **powers** and authorities, he made a public spectacle of them, triumphing over them by the cross (Colossians 2:15)". Again we read, "With angels, authorities and **powers** in submission to him (1 Peter 3:22)."

Spiritual Forces

In the writings to the Corinthians, we read, "For the weapons of our warfare are not of the flesh but have divine power to destroy strongholds (2 Corinthians 10:4,)." Furthermore, we read in the book of Daniel, we read "Do not be afraid, Daniel. . . . However, the prince of the Persian kingdom resisted me twenty-one days. Then Michael, one of the chief princes, came to help me, because I was detained there with the king of Persia.[14] Now I have come to explain to you what will happen to your people in the future, for the vision concerns a time yet to come (Daniel 10:12-14)"

Satan the Prince of this world

Jesus gave Lucifer the title, "prince of this world, "because he is the leader and most powerful fallen angel. Jesus called him a liar. Why does Jesus call him prince? Because there are other spiritual forces who follow Lucifer (John 16:11)." "Now is the time for judgment on **this world**; now the **prince of this world** will be driven out (John 12:31). "I will not say much more to you, for the **prince of this world** is coming. He has no hold over me (John 14:30 I)." "Be alert and of sober mind. Your enemy the devil prowls around like a roaring lion looking for someone to devourl (1Peter 5:8)."

Satan is the King over fallen angels

Satan has many names as you can see. He is the devil but he is also called the king of darkness. He is also pictured as a lion like Jesus. Peter correctly says Satan is looking for someone to devour. If you were to travel around the world, many believers blame him for everything. That is giving him too much power. He does not do every act of evil, other evil angels do. Even humans commit evil without the help of Satan. It is true that he is the chief organizer of evil empires all over the world. He never created anything (Revelation 12: 7-9).

The Two Great Angels-Michael and Gabriel

There are two big names among elect angels: Michael and Gabriel. If Michael shows up it is bad news. However, if Gabriel shows up it is good news. Michael was the protector of Israel. That means he can put up a fight against Lucifer (Jude and Revelation 12:7). Do you realize now why the rankings exist? There are angels with more influence.

Both Gabriel and Michael are archangels with different responsibilities. Satan was in the same class as Michael and Gabriel. However, I am of the opinion that he had the highest responsibility than either one of them (all angels reported to him since he was a chief a guardian Cherub)

Satan's Strategy-Just lie

1. He lied to angels who followed him.
2. He lied to Eve and led to the original sin
3. He tried lie to Jesus who caught him at his lies
4. He lies to people all the time

Within the organization of angels, there are four categories of angels. The term, "star" refers to all angelic (good or evil) beings. It simply means heavenly beings. However, evil angels no longer dwell in heaven. Below are the terminologies that apply to angels.

Cherubim, Seraphim's, living creatures (extraordinary angels supposedly pictured with "wings (not really)" in visions or dreams or trances. The above depict the most powerful class of angels as I explained the rankings above. A few words regarding the living creatures. All these are angels depicted in animal form.

The living Creatures

In Ezekiel, Isaiah and Revelation and a few other places, we read about certain angels described as winged creatures. Winged creatures are the same class as living creatures. They are described with certain properties that seem to different from the rest of angels. People have taken interest in descriptions of "wings" and other sophisticated parts that capture our attention." The description given in certain angels in the particular Scriptures have left people believe that angels have wings. However, what the Scriptures is describing are the potentialities of angels. By using animal, and birds' attributes, the observer (prophet) can easily understand what he knows about the characteristics that relate to the animals so described. The prophets did the same thing when they give us the picture of God in a language we could understand. To give us a closer understanding of God's invisible attributes, the Bible describes him in terms of birds (chicken), animals (lion or bear) humans (hands, or feet) characteristics. The question we ask; what role do these animal's parts play in their existence? Take for example an eagle's wings; what is it for? A lion, what is it well known for? If we know what these birds or animals and people do with their characteristics, that is the point the narrator is conveying. God has no eyes; but he is portrayed as seeing using physical eyes. The larger question is, why use these characteristics? The simple answer is that God is Spirit. In a simple language, he is invisible and so are the angels who are spirits. The prophet is a human being. He cannot see spirits with a naked eye. God who knows all things creates a picture to the prophet through the means of a vision or trance. God then describes the attributes of angels by appealing to things the prophet is familiar with. Every place where we see these creatures with funny parts is in dreams, trances, or visions. At those times, the prophet or apostle himself always sees these creatures when he is *IN the spirit.* Go back and read every Scripture that talk about creatures with wings, eyes, wheels and so on. The person who sees these creatures is always in the spirit. That is the most important clue in your interpretation. The point of figures of speech is so that we get the meaning but do not take the picture language that is given literally. Great interpreters of Scripture, whom I respect a lot, have gone wrong on this point because they forgot to put these descriptions in their proper context. Let me then explain these Scriptures in general.

The first obvious question we need to unlock is, are these real living creature or the author is giving us the attributes of angels? Do angels have wings for real? In Isaiah 6:2; Ezekiel 1 and Revelation 4:6. What would be the function of wings for these living creatures? Where do they ever fly since they are always in the presence of God? Why do they have wheels? What are wheels for? If you believe they have wings, then believe also that they have wheels and eyes everywhere. Then believe too that in heaven they have material stuff. Be consistent.

Unfortunately, I know you are disappointed, the living creatures we read about with wings and wheels do not exist in heaven at all (flesh and blood cannot inherit the kingdom of God, 1 Cor. 15)). Heaven was created for spirits and they are the hosts (Psalm 148:2) of heaven. Hosts of heaven have always been spirit beings who do not need food. These creatures do not have wings. They do not need that and they do not live in material form but spirit. Let me says it one more time; the living creatures with crazy looks are always beholden in visions but not in real life. Every time a real angel appears before people-they are never with wings. If this makes sense, it will remove all the confusions some theologians have erroneously taught. None of the creatures have ever been seen by naked eyes. John who wrote the book of Revelation and saw the things he wrote through the spirit not in real life. What he saw were depictions of a particular truth in material form so that he could relate to it. It is critical to take note of that and ask yourself why. What attribute are such Scriptures communicating? We need to ask that question first.

Visions

Visions in most cases are metaphorical language given to us for a special message. We also know God is described in human and animal terms in order to give us a special message. To maintain a consistence method of interpretations, we should lay more emphasis on these descriptions as symbolical language.

Take the Scripture and just examine what it says: Let us consider Isaiah 6, as an example. "In the year that King Uzziah died, I saw the Lord, high and exalted, seated on a throne; and the train of his robe filled the temple.² Above him were seraphim, each with six wings: With two wings they covered their faces, with two they covered their feet, and with two they were flying.³ And they were calling to one another: "Holy, holy, holy is the LORD Almighty; the whole earth is full of his glory." At the sound of their voices the doorposts and thresholds shook and the temple was filled with smoke. "Woe to me!" I cried. "I am ruined! For I am a man of unclean lips, and I live among a people of unclean lips, and my eyes have seen the King, the LORD Almighty." Then one of the seraphim flew to me with a live coal in his hand, which he had taken with tongs from the altar.⁷ With it he touched my mouth and said, "See, this has touched your lips; your guilt is taken away and your sin atoned for."

Here is a question, "which Lord did Isaiah see seated on the throne? God is Spirit. Remember that vision came to Isaiah before Jesus took on human form. The Bible says no man has ever seen God. What did Isaiah see then?

He saw God seated on the throne. To be consisted with the symbolisms, it is proper to describe the rest of the hosts of (angels) heaven also in material form. That is the most logical thing to do. If he has seen God seated, those who are with him should be normalized in material terms as well. The big question then is this; what is God trying to tell Isaiah to make it very clear that he had a message from God? First, the message was not for Isaiah, it was for his people the Israelites.

The message was to Israel before the era of grace. Did Isaiah see the Father or the Son seated on the throne with his naked eyes? Alternatively, in a symbolic language the prophet is merely saying, the Lord rules as a king above all the affairs of human beings. Surely, does the Father literary sit on a physical throne; does he? Then the Scripture has lied that says no one has seen God. How big was that throne that God sat on? Why do I ask that question? The reason I ask that question is that the same Bible says nothing can contain God (1Kings 8:27). The highest heaven cannot contain God. Where did he sit and what heaven was he in. If we say that this is figure of speech, then the whole scene the prophet is describing is figure of speech.

128

Does the Father Literally Sit on a Throne

Everything in that Scripture is symbolic languages of how earthly kings sits and rule on thrones. That is easy message for the people who live on earth to understand. Even though God is in heaven, he rules. He rules with his angels who are his messengers. It is easy for the servant of the Lord to understand the message if it is relayed in human experience. The Lord gives to Isaiah a familiar picture so that the people will understand the message not that the Father of Jesus is literary on the throne. It must be a very BIG throne. If this message came after the resurrection, I would entertain the idea that he saw Jesus on the throne. However, this was before the incarnation. Jesus had not yet taken on human form at that moment and therefore it cannot refer to Jesus at all.

If the vision that Isaiah saw pertains to symbolic language, the Father seated, then whole context is symbolic as well? "Above him were seraphim, each with six wings: With two wings they covered their faces, with two they covered their feet, and with two they were flying.[3] And they were calling to one another." Why cover faces? To convey the holiness of God otherwise what is the point. Fly to go where! Flying is a sign of mobility of birds, Isaiah understand flying. However, the message is that angels of God can move from point one to point two. The angels are able to move at any time when as they are commanded. They function as persons. The Scriptures explain spiritual stuff in symbolic language to help us understand the message. They have faces. What do faces remind you of? It reminds us of persons who have faces. These spirits have personalities. That is the point. God is wise. He knows we cannot see in the spiritual realm but he cannot fail to communicate what he wants. He uses visions, dreams, and trances to convey a message in familiar things in order for us to understand it.

Sophisticated picture of living creatures

The point is that angels do not have wings nor do they have any of these features. The author is giving us the work that these angels can do (wings are a picture of mobility of flying. However, angels do not necessarily fly; they appear. Spirits only appear they do not fly. Material things can fly. Spirits do not fly. The picture of these living creatures only tells us of their potentiality. They are able to perform their responsibility by looking at their potentiality imbued by their Boss. If the Lord were to use spiritual language to describe the potentiality of these spiritual beings, Isaiah would be at a loss and he could not convey the message to us. It would be hard for a human mind to capture such vastness and his immeasurable wealth of wisdom to convey to us what certain angels can do. The Lord gives this picture so that we can appreciate the wealth of his wisdom and intelligence. The creatures have amazing attributes that we can never understand unless they are given to us in picture form using familiar objects. There are no such animals or creatures in heaven. Heaven is the abode of spirits. Angels are the living creatures referred to in such Scriptures not real blooded creatures with wheels in their wings.

The Father of Jesus is Spirit and does not possess human features as such and so are his angels. The Scripture is clear that says angels are spirits. In order to show us his unsearchable wisdom of the potentiality of powerful angels, God gave Isaiah vivid images in vision form in order to inform Israelites what angels are capable of. The depiction of angels with these amazing attributes only serve to convey their abilities. In the context quoted above, God is display attributes of angels in animal form. Human beings are familiar with animal characteristics. We do not know angelic characteristics. The same would apply in the story of Ezekiel and Revelation. Angels do not have wings as such because they are spirits. They do not need wings for flying either. There is no reason angels would need wings. Where do angels live? Where is the home of angels?

Angelic home

There is another argument as to the abode of angels? Do they live in the first, second, or third heaven? My former professor argued that they live in a second heaven. All elect angels are holy. They became elect when they chose not to sin or follow Satan. All those that followed Satan are already condemned. They condemned themselves when they followed Satan. Angels that sinned and followed Satan became known as demons or evil angels. The angels who did not sin but remained faithful to God became known as elect angels. All angels were holy before sin was found in them. Elect angels are still the current hosts of heaven. Heaven will always be a home for angels not human beings. Only spiritual beings can exist in heaven. The creature we read above are angels (spirits) and serve God daily. There is no darkness among spirits. Therefore there is no light nor darkness in heaven. Nighttime does not exist up there neither does day. How did some angels lose their abode in heaven? How did that happen?

How it happened

Evil entered heaven first before it found its way on earth. Angels made personal decisions to follow God or rebel against him. God did not go round naming some angels as elect and others as demons. It never happened that way. It was based on the decisions each angel made. Every angel had an opportunity independently to either obey God or not. To put it another way, upon obedience or disobedience, the terms "elect and demons "were coined. They are not original. Original things were very good including Satan and demons. Elect angels residence is in heaven (their original home -hosts of heaven). Those that rebelled have no home and hence roam about. Some of these angels went beyond their domain. I will explain later. What happened among angels is what happened with Adam and Eve. It was until Adam and Eve made a choice that we were introduced to evil. Let me continue on angels. Which heaven do angels live? Is it in the first heaven? Is it in the second heaven or third. There are three heavens, which we know. Where do angels live? Does God dwell in third heaven or higher than that? The Scriptures clearly states that there is apparently even higher than ALL the Heavens and that is where Jesus apparently ascended (Ephesians 4:9-11). That sounds true because before he created the heavens where did he dwell. Let us read the Scriptures, "'Heaven is my throne, and the earth is my footstool. What kind of house will you build for me? "Or where will my resting place be (Acts 7:49)? Notice here its singular-"heaven," not heavens. If God made everything, where was his throne before then? "Has not my hand made all these things (Genesis 1:1)? God created the heavens and the earth. Better yet, God says, "the earth is his footstool. Where can we find his feet (Acts 7:50)?"

We read in Hebrews, "Such a high priest truly meets our need—one who is holy, blameless, pure, set apart from sinners, exalted above the heavens (Heb. 7:26). Agrees with Ephesians 4:9-11 and affirms that Jesus was somewhere before the heavens were made. So where is Jesus? God has never said that the third heaven is his throne. The Bible says that heaven is where his throne is. That means he does not necessarily live in heaven. If Jesus passed through the heavens where did he Go? Therefore, you must agree that metaphors mean something. That takes us to another hot issues regarding angels. The title of my book, Do Angels Smooch?

Were these Smooching Angels?

One of the thorniest issues in conspiracy theories in biblical history is recorded in the book of Genesis. We read, *"When human beings began to increase in number on the earth and daughters were born to them,[2] the sons of God saw that the daughters of humans were beautiful, and they married any of them they chose . . . " The Nephilim were on the earth in those days—and also afterward—when the sons of God went to the daughters of humans and had children by them. They were the heroes of old, men of renown (Genesis 6:1-4).*

First, the term, Nephilim; it does not refer to children born in the intermarriage between children of God and daughters of men. The Bible does not say that. What the Bible implies is that these Nephilim's were in existence during the intermarriage of children of God and daughters of men. The Bible says," the Nephilim were on earth in those days (during this intermarriage and after intermarriage)-and also afterwards." Second, Genesis chapter six gives us reasons why the flood was inevitable. What happened in Genesis chapter six led that led to one of the greatest catastrophes in human history.

Who were the Nephilim? The Nephilim were "heroes of old, men of renown." The term Nephilim refers to males only. That sheds light to dispute what some assume that Nephilim were the product of intermarriages between angels and women. The intermarriage cannot produce only males. Nephilim in the Scripture before (Genesis 6) us and in Numbers (Numbers 13) always refers to males. The term Nephilim means giants. The author seems to know what happened in Noah's time and the wilderness period. That is quite a long stretch of time. Only the person who was there during Noah's day as well as Moses's day would know that it is the same breed of humans. Those who think that the copulation of women and angels produced Nephilim will have a hard time explaining Number 13 where we find the same giants who are always male. I do not take that position. Follow my arguments below and determine what makes sense.

We know that Noah did not write the book of Genesis. We also know that he is the only person and his family that survived the flood. The Nephilim of Noah's day perished under the flood. We know that because only Noah and his family survived. However, these breed of giants showed up hundreds of years later after the flood. After the flood, there were no more intermarriage between angels and women. Yet Nephilim still showed up. My point is that these giants were normal products of human beings. The children that were born by the intermarriages of angels and women, all perished under the flood. After hundreds of years later, we read, "We saw the Nephilim there the descendants of Anak come from the Nephilim, we seemed like grasshoppers in our own eyes, and we looked the same to them (Numbers 17:4)." That is what the Bible meant afterwards in Genesis 6:4. Goliath is considered a giant (1 Samuel 17:4). We need to see that difference. Mingling of angels and women did not produce Nephilim.

Genesis 6 account has been debated since the dawn of biblical history. Almost every religious Jewish leader believed without debate that these sons of God were angels. I do too. Even during the early church, most church Fathers concurred with Jewish interpretations. Today we have a number of differing views among great thinkers in bibliology, theology and to some extent secular philosophers. They have plunged in the debate of Genesis 6. Some views could easily be debunked. The debate heavily hinges between angels and the line of Seth. If the story in Genesis 6 checks out to be true, and that these were angels, what would that mean? On a lighter note, one wonders at the beauty of women such that even celestial beings left heaven for them. Angels undertook that huge sacrifice. We read some intriguing narratives concerning some patriarchal fathers whose wives were very beautiful to the extent that their own husbands lied about them for fear of being killed. How beautiful could women be? We cannot ignore that line; they saw that the daughters of men were beautiful! Contextually, it can only mean someone who had never seen women before.

Angels are not omnipresent. Furthermore, they live in heaven until all the time. Unless they have a mission to undertake, that is when they come to earth. Women have always existed concurrently with men. If it were just one man that expressed that sentiment that women were beautiful, I would buy the belief that it was the line of Seth. The context suggests that it was a group of sons of God. Their first impression when they saw daughters of men it seems that they were intoxicated with their beauty. These Sons of God were impressed when they saw daughters of men. The context also clearly states, daughters of men. That includes Sethites. What is strange about Sethites men marrying within the group of women who they bore? It does not make sense. Furthermore, there was no classification of people then as holy group or unholy. The statement itself says a lot; "saw daughters of men." Sethites were always in the presence of women. They grow up on earth together. They always saw their daughters (daughters of men). Furthermore, there was no law yet that forbade marry from a particular group of people tribes. Marrying within the family was normal even during Abraham's times. Noah's time was earlier than Abraham was. Some interpret the Scriptures either using human traditions, Mosaic Law, or using New Testament lenses. You need to be careful in doing that. To interpret Genesis 6, you have to look at the times of Noah first and foremost. How many people perished under the flood? What happened to Sethites so called holy line? Many have avoided considering Noahic context. They have employed their own bias to explain away what is basic and straightforward. Were all Sethites women wicked? Only Noah's family survived. We need to interpret the Scripture within the period of Noah. During Noah's time, people could marry anybody or even within their own families. There was no communal faith then but personal. There were no church buildings at all. God said nothing about Lot's daughters who slept with their father. Incest was not in view neither was marrying non-believers a known doctrine. Incest and other sexual sins became apparent during Mosaic Law. The Mosaic code came into effect over a thousand years after the account of Genesis 6. We cannot interpret Scripture using modern lenses because the narrative in Genesis 6 is grotesque. The best interpretation that suits the context is Sons of God would mean angels. I will let that sink in. I would like to think a bit more about the beauty of these women. Beauty enticed these celestial beings to fall in love, a thing that was not permitted to them. The angels in Genesis 6 had a chance to smooch daughters of men.

Are women that beautiful such that angels married them?

The intriguing question we need to consider is, how beautiful where the women of ante-diluvian period? How beautiful can women be? How do we define beauty? Some say beauty is in the beholder. In my opinion, my daughters are the most beautiful women on the entire planet. Even the Bible agrees with me (Psalms 139). These women attracted celestial beings because of their beauty and led the world to a decisive end. We live in times of pageants where the parade of beautiful women has become a lucrative business. These women were naturally beautiful without being polished up with modern cosmetics. What is in the appealing beauty of a woman? I secretly adore my girls and very jealousy of them. To me no man can qualify to marry my beautiful girls. It is difficulty to let go, however, I know they are God's possession and not mine. Therefore, I might grudgingly let go, but I will not say that definitively. Angels saw what most men take for granted; they saw that the daughters of men were beautiful and forfeited their highest position in the universe (heaven) in order to be with women. Just to come and smooch the daughters of men. Did these angels even pay the dowry price (lobola)? On the other hand, was it free for all? Whatever you think about women, some angels thought that they were beautiful and came and married them. It is appropriate to enquire whether angels smooch. Let us look at that.

PART 6

Do Angels Smooch? Even Today

Sons of God in the books of Job and Genesis mean angels. Some of the angels in their rebellion against God involved having sexual activities with women. That was not just rebelling but also going outside their domain of operation. Jude gives us an insight to confirm that interpretation, "And the angels who did not keep their positions of authority but abandoned their proper dwelling (Jude 1:6)." Angels were not supposed to marry unfortunately, they did. They did something worse than other angels did. They married outside their authority (meaning they abandoned "their proper dwelling "or domain). They married women from the earth (their dwelling was in heaven). Just as Adam and Eve were not allowed to eat from the tree in the middle of the garden, but they did anyway. In the same way, angels are not permitted to marry that group did anyway. Angels are not given in marriage. What is the simple meaning of that? It simply means they are not allowed to marry. The fact that they are not allowed to do that, tells us something else; it means they can break or obey the command. The Bible does not say it is impossible for angels to marry. Here is what we find in the book of Matthew, "At the resurrection people will neither marry nor be given in marriage; they will be like the angels in heaven (Matthew 22: 30),." Does that Scripture say that people at the resurrection will not have reproductive organs so that they are like angels? It just says "people will neither marry nor be given in marriage." Put it bluntly, marriage will not be permitted after the resurrection. But why compare people to angels if it is impossible for angels to get involved in sexual activities? Therefore, angels are not allowed to marry. Why forbid something if it is impossible to perform an action? God has never told angels, do not try to become like Me. He has never said that because he knows it is futile to try to become like Him. The devil tried, and he failed. If there is a possibility of performing an action, then there is also a chance to forbid it. That is the only logical meaning. Angels were not permitted to marry and hence all

141

angels appear to be males. As you can deduce, when they saw women, some disobeyed the command. My philosophy on such matters has been; whatever is prohibited, gives rise to a possibility of disobedience. For example, if God had tied the hands of Eve and closed her mouth, there would be no need to tell her not to eat from the tree. It would be impossible for her to perform that action. If the Bible had said it is impossible for angels to marry, then there is no need even to say they are not permitted to marry. That would be redundancy. You only forbid something that has likelihood to happen. Alternatively forbid something that has a possibility of acting contrary to the command.

Hosts of heaven and hosts of earth have been given different expectations and practices. Human beings are permitted to marry in this age while angels are not permitted. To have intermarriages between angels and human is to create a third category God never intended. That explains why God wiped out the byproduct of that union, by the use of the flood. All the children that were born from that union, perished. The angels, who were involved in that union, are still bound. It is the only group of fallen angels who are not permitted to roam the earth again. I have argued in my other papers one important principle; whatever God clearly forbids (either angels or people) the opposite is possible. It means that there is a possibility of performing that action. God does not forbid anything that is impossible to perform. God has never forbidden human beings to become dogs. As human beings, don't we sometimes behave worse than dogs? However, we cannot become actual dogs. So why worst time talking about the impossible. God only forbids things that capable of being disobeyed. Furthermore, when such a direct command is disobeyed, it carries with it hefty consequences. Adam and Eve by their disobedience plunged all human race in the present predicament (death to all human race). We are dying to this day. Likewise, those particular angels that went further in their rebellion, they are bound. They are the only class of angels who are not allowed to roam the earth any more until the judgment day. In fact, they cannot do it again because they are bound. They remain bound until the final Day of Judgment.

The Scripture referenced in second Peter has a better explanation why this particular group of angels has been excluded from roaming the earth. We have all sinned, including the devil and yet we are freely enjoying some form of freedom. Telling lies is the MO of the devil. Nevertheless, the devil still roams in spite of his sins. The reason he can still do that is because he did not participate to do the unthinkable, marrying daughters of men. He will still be judged but at least for now he is on the loose. The devil never slept with women but these angels did. The books of second Peter and Jude are the best commentary on Genesis chapter six in the whole Bible. Let me reference it in this context: *"For if God did not spare angels when they sinned, but sent them to hell, putting them in chains of darkness to be held for judgment. . . (2 Peter 2:4-7). "Jude reads, " And the angels who did not keep their positions of authority but abandoned their proper dwelling—these he has kept in darkness, bound with everlasting chains for judgment on the great Day* (Jude 6). *You* ask yourself why only these angels? Why not all angels who sinned? The only best explanation is that these angels did the unthinkable. First, they descended to the earth. Second, they got married and produced children instead of staying where they belonged, heaven. Thirdly, they abandoned their position of authority. Fourth, by marrying daughters of men, they thereby polluted human seed.

Let me explain what is going on why the punishment was severe. Bear in mind, unlike wild animals; angels have the abilities to retain all human attributes. That is, they possess male biological functions (Genesis 18). In their spirit state (authority), they cannot function as we do. Notwithstanding, they are the only created beings endued with the ability to be spirits, and humans when necessary. They have that potentiality of being humans and spirits that we cannot attain. They have the ability to use human voice. We cannot use their language or voice. All this to just to say, they can transition from spirit to human form in an instance. When they do that, they retain all male biological attributes. At that point, they are persons standing next to you. They can do anything that humans do. That is why it was possible to bear children. It follows therefore that if they could bear children by having sex with women, they could smooch as well (smooching is part of intimacy). There is absolutely no immoral render that differently. Contrast that with holy angels. They are called elect; they are named that way because they refrained from sinning. God did not force any angel to be on his side if that where the case no angel or humans would have sinned. Furthermore, the early church held this point. Surely, logic tells me that if a person can sleep with a woman, what stops them from smooching. There is a high possibility that some angels in the past smooched women when they had that relationship. Here is what we know. Smooching is usually associated with sexual activities unlike traditional or biblical kissing. Cheek kissing is common in many cultures of the world. Normal kissing on the cheek is a formal way of greeting in most Middle Eastern culture and elsewhere. Nevertheless, angelic participation in smooching is unheard of today. That is where I found the story in Genesis 6 hard to believe as I reflect back. In any case, how does one know if it is a real angel who is smooching since they appear in real human form? We face that difficulty part today. It seems to me that it is out of question for holy angels to smooch people today. That season is over. It may have happened in the past but not today. Let me briefly give a simple theological response. The reason is obvious if you have followed the arguments that have been presented so far. For one thing, each angel has personally made an irrevocable decision either to follow God or not. In other words, there will never be another rebellion among angelic beings. Therefore, the possibility of smooching is completely out of question. Having said that, here is something I can affirmatively state; holy angels can kiss any person on the cheek even today, but you will never know (camouflaged). Angelic kissing on cheeks is possible if an angel was sent to people whose manners and customs involve kissing as a way of greeting. When angels take on human nature, they participate in any holy activities that people are involved in. If the angel fails to observe such customs, it may raise suspicions. It could also be misinterpreted as insulting or disrespecting that culture (if you have read the Bible, even our Lord Jesus their Boss was kissed while in human form). That is the last thing any angel on a good mission would do. Furthermore it would defeat their most important objective; appearing incognito. Our discussion on smooching arose because of the lyrics or movies and other literature that have insinuated angelic involvement in human emotions. The truth is that angels are all around us. They are busy helping us in many ways. The only thing they are not allowed to do is participate in our intimate sexual activities. They are not allowed to go that far. That does not means we ourselves are not interested. Human nature is the craziest among all living creatures. The Sodomites where very much interested in having sex with angels. However, the holy angels could not allow it. That is their (angels) stance now. They are here and can do anything that normal human beings do except smooching. Do angels smooch? Some did long ago. We know that the ones that still roam around do not.

Conclusion

What do you think about angels after having read this book? President Trump can tell you about Angels Moms he met. Some musicians have produced songs about angels. While other have made movies; Charles's Angels or Touched by an Angel and much more. What is your story that you know or have heard relating to angels? Have you assumed that all these are mere metaphors or myths? Is there is truth to them?

Many people around the world have conceded that angels do exist. A number of people further accept that angels have influence on our communities and continue do so even now. From the discussions in the book, it seems that the primary work of angels is helping people in need. It is correct to say, angels exist to serve both God and human beings. That is the primary reason why angels exist. What is clear is that good angels do not serve their own interests. That is the main difference between holy and evil angels. Evil angels and the devil serve their own interests. Angels were created to serve, that is why they are not permitted to marry. The number of angels remains the same. Angels were never born. Each angel is a direct creation of God. Angels have no relatives.

We now know that angels do not marry or build houses. From the beginning to this day, their sole purpose is to serve God and people. These sentient beings work night and day without sleep. We never hear that angels are tired and that they are taking a nap. That is not in their MO. From the studies, we have come to learn that good angels are not our enemies at all. Fallen angels known as demons are the enemies of people. Some problems and conflicts we face are instigated by the evil angels who have no homes of their own. Demons and Satan were kicked out of their original home. Right now, all they do is just wonder about aimlessly. Since they are spirits, they can indwell a person by force. We call that demon possession. They are very jealous of our position. Their goal is perpetual hatred of people. Their top priority is to move us to hate God. They have nothing to lose, we do. We can lose our relationship with God. Fallen angels have done worse things than just terrorizing your teeth. The story that took place in Zambia maybe true or fiction, but the larger point in that story and many others is that evil angels have infiltrated our dwelling places. That is the reality we should embrace and be on the lookout. Some evil angels including their boss the devil contribute to our suffering. Good angels on the other hand bring great fortunes and comfort to people as we have seen in the stories above. Angels are sometimes sent to protect people in danger besides bringing good news. That person who just showed up from nowhere might be an angel who came to minister to you. Angels help people and nations in many ways. How would you like to fight an invisible enemy who does not even get tired? Fighting invisible enemies is a big challenge that is why we need invisible allies to help us. That is why being hospitable helps. Hospitality can invite more angels on your side.

The prospect of entertaining an angel is one of the fascinating stories ever encouraged. The probabilities of entertaining an angel are even greater if you are hospitable to strangers. Such gesture of being hospitable should stem from a good motive to yield positive results. People who are hospitable stand a better chance of entertaining angels. To have a good angel visit you, is like having God himself coming in your home, imagine that. A holy angel always represents God. That means if a holy angel came to your home, it is like having a personal attention by the Creator of the universe Himself. Meditate on that. We are talking about very serious issues.

Let me give a word of advice to all of us. Do not expect to see a personality with wings coming to see you. No human being in the history of the world has ever seen an angel with wings with naked eyes. Real angels do not have wings. Real angels always appear in human form. That is why I spent time explaining their attire. Besides, if angels were to appear with wings, the whole world would go crazy. The internet would crush forever. A real angel will look exactly like any normal human being probably wearing some jeans and flip-flops. Another hint to keep in mind is that, a real angel always appears in the form of a male person. Remember and write these two points down. Let me repeat myself; angels do not have wings and always appears as males.

That is how they manage to minister to us and we think it was the Joneses. Forget about Hollywood that has portrayed angels with wings and sometimes as females (no offence to our beautiful women). That is a work of fiction. It has been said that when you do something repeatedly, it will be taken as true. Some argue and say the Bible talks about angels. Yes, the Bible does talk about angels with wings or winged creatures, but in what context? Without exception, it is either in a vision, in spirit or trance. The point is that the visions or trances are only appear in heavens (check that from the Bible). Ask yourself, why? Because if God were to make angels appear in their nature (spirits), how could a naked eye see them. God is helping us understand the attributes of angels. They do not have wings, wheels, eyes all over them.

What is the function of wings? Wings are for flying. The mode of movements by spirits is called appearances. Angels do not fly, they appear. I have tried to emphasize that point in order to alert us to the reality we face. Angels will always come in human form. I gave you some leading points how to determine if that person who came to you was an angel.

Imagine people in your neighborhood hearing that an angel is visiting you. If people heard that an angel was visiting you, the chaos that would arise would be unstoppable. The commotion that would ensue may lead to death of many people. I am sure you now appreciate why angels come incognito. There is a gossip going round saying angels are very handsome. I doubt that. We have no evidence to prove that. How could a person know that it was an angel that visited them? Unless an angel discloses himself, the way angel Gabriel did. On the other hand, we wonder why the people in Gomorrah were obsessed with the angels that visited Lot. They must have been looking handsome. That is why in Sodom and Gomorrah men were desperate to have sex with them. When they appear as handsome men, there is such an attraction to them. However, we cannot conclude that in every case they appear with handsome faces. That too would defeat their purpose of camouflage. As you can imagine it is not a small thing to be visited by an angel. In fact, it is more beneficial than having all the leaders of the world including kings and queens, come to your house. Angels are sometimes camouflaged in human bodies to avoid un necessary attention. Could that open a door to smooching? Today no holy angel can smooch anyone. They learned a good lesson from what happened to their colleagues who smooched women. Apparently, some angels smooched women a long time ago. What is important now is to continue showing hospitality to strangers because in so doing you may entertain holy angels. Here is a thought for us before you put the book down. Right now as I write, an angel is visiting somebody somewhere on earth. That somebody could be you in the future if you are hospitable. From that day on, your life may take on a new meaning. I am sharing with you things that matter in life. Serving others has greater benefits, to God and to you.

What about angels and us

Have you noticed something in our world? We talk about God. We talk about angels. We talk about animals and insects. We talk about other creatures under the seas. Then we go to in animate things across our planets including known and unknown stars. In this book, I have focused on angels concerning our emotions. In particular, as it relates to, wardrobe, emotions and sexual activities. We face these very real issues. Angels are real entities that surround and influence our cultures indirectly. Angels are important and that is why the good book advises us to be hospitable so that we may have a chance to be visited by an angel. In as much as I have talked more about angels, do you notice something? In as much as we talk about God, do you notice something? In as much as we talk about the universe, do you notice something? In as much as we talk about dogs, cats, horses or animals in general do you notice something. In as much as we talk about Satan and his angels do you notice something? Everything has *something to do with us* or we have something to do with them. Do you realize that we are the focus of *all things that exists?* Think about that. Let us all agree that God created us, of course we believe that by faith. Even though God created us, we are the focus of all that exists. We take care of the earth. We take care of the dead. We take care of the living. We take care of our animals. Yes, God exists but no one will refute that we are the focus of all that exists. God wants us to love him. God wants us to serve him. God wants us to behave ourselves. Satan and his evil angels are pursuing us relentlessly day and night. Viruses want to destroy us. Domesticated animals want us to take care of them. We beautify the earth. Everything up there in the galaxies has direct relationship with us. The Sun sends it rays to us. The Moon reflects its light on our earth. The stars display their beauty to us. Everything out there seems to be related to us one-way or another. *So how could one refute that good angels have no direct dealings with us.* That is impossible. Good angels are the liaison between God and humans. We must be very careful though, at no point are we supposed to worship angels. Worship is reserved only for the Godhead (the Father, the Son and the Holy Spirit). However, never under estimate the work of angels among us. If you are holding this book in your hands, one idea you should take away is that good and evil angels surround us and both of them have *something to do with us.* Angel's attention is not on their fellow angels, God, or even animals, but people.

My point is we are surrounded by the sentient beings that run between God and us. Ask yourself, why are they here? What are they accomplishing between their Boss and us? God does not need angels. We do. God is everywhere and he can do anything he desires in a flash of second without the help of angels. He existed without angels. *Angels were created for our sake.* What would God want from angels? Absolutely nothing. Angels were created with the potentiality of transforming into human beings instantly and within a second be able to retain their spirit form. They are there for us even though God gave them another job of worship. However, worship is not a big deal. Everything on earth can be compelled to worship God. Jesus can command stones to worship him. The most important job for angels is to run errands directed at human beings. Angels do not run errands to fellow angels but to people. Here is another point. *Angels are the closest point we can touch God.* Their Boss (the Father) has never materialized into flesh and blood, but angels do. These sentient beings know exactly how their Boos looks like. To touch angels while in human form is the closest we can ever touch their Boss. Other than that, the Son of God is the only exact representation of the Boss of angels. To touch him is to touch the living God. "If you have seen me, you have seen the Father (John 14:9)," said Jesus. Do you get the point why being hospital to strangers could bring you closer to God? Why is that? Because their Boss is the only one, who makes decisions where to send his angels. To have an angel in your home is equivalent to have God himself in your presence (Gabriel said I stand in the presence of God"). That could change your life forever.

Angels do not say it is written; but rather, this what God says

God always sends his angels in human form. However, angels come in the spiritual form from heaven and then transform into persons on earth. Nevertheless, they move about in a spirit form from one point to another. They just appear and disappear (case for Philip). God, as God per se, will never ever materialize in human form except through his Son. However, remember, the Son of God in human form can only be in one place at any given time. Listen to this; God manifests himself physically to people through his angels. That is the only way we meet God physically. He is Spirit. Talking to an angel is talking with God himself. They do not come in their own names. They always come in the name of God. Angels do *not say it is written; they say this what God says*. Do not under estimate visits of angels. Angelic visit is the same thing as God focusing on you exclusively. Angels stand in the very presence of God. When we talk about angelic visitation, we are actually talking about God giving you special attention. Angels used their potentiality to transform from spirit mode to physical mode. The angel who married women were in human form which enabled to copulate with women. Women were not aware that their husbands were angels. These angels took on human form, which they used to smooch women they had married and had children by them. Fortunately, the group of people that were involved in that scandal perished under the flood. Since angels cannot live in human form continuously, these rebellious angels retained their spirit and did not perish under the flood. Nevertheless, God was able to restrict (bound) their movement. That group of angels who married women is still bound as we speak. The word bound is used loosely to mean restricted from movement (roaming the earth) the way other evil angels are able to do.

The face of a person is the face of God

Angels are more powerful than humans' beings. However, they are not made in the image of God. Only humans' beings among all living things were created in the image of God. Yet when angels visit a person, they represent God himself as I stated above. There is something else we need to know about people and angels. An angel in human form that stands before any person presents the face of God. That is why Jesus said if you have seen me, you have seen the Father. Jesus is the exact representation of God in human form. In as much as angels will never be in the shoes of Jesus, however, they are the closest physical representation of God before any person. A spirit can be represented in material form. The catch phrase is "represented." Angels represent God in material form. I am not emphasizing Jesus right now but pointing out how powerful angelic representation of God is. That representation is not beheld in the spirit form, but in human form. Now follow the next statement I am going to make. The evil angels in Genesis 6 would have tarnished the image of God through their union with women. The byproduct of angels and women did not possess the image of God. They were not the seed of humanity per se. God's image was tarnished in their offspring because their sex union was unnatural. Previously the boss to evil angels wanted to become like God, He failed. The angels in Genesis 6 by copulating with women would have corrupted human seed and inadvertently tarnish the image of God in humans. There would have been two kinds of people. The first that came through human seed by natural selection. The second would have come between the union of created spirits and human flesh. God would not have it. Of all angels that sinned, only that group of angels who cohabited with women has been bound. I believe that Satan did not participate in that form of rebellion because if he had, God would have done to him what he did to the other group. God is no respecter of persons. Satan led a group of angels in rebellion but he did not lead them to have sexual union with women. Their sin was beyond the pale. Women, who participated in sexual union including smooching, have long been exterminated. Their offspring perished under the flood. Noah had to start a new generation of people free from such contamination. Do you wonder why the following narrative was given? Let me quote it, "These are the clans of Noah's sons, according to their lines of descent, within their nations. From these the nations spread out over the earth after the flood." That paragraph was done on purpose in order to make sure we get the picture that there were no other nations were on earth except Noah and his family. That is to assure us that the rebellion in Genesis 6 was exterminated forever. There is no longer a possibility of angels smooching as I have explained earlier. Do angels smooch? They did but not anymore. Who were ministering before and after the flood? It was angels. I know we boast of our great exploits as human beings. Like I said, I personally applaud and appreciate any work well done by any human being regardless of their faith. Whoever they are. I am sure you too do not like the vices we see in our countries all over the world. The Lord Jesus said, do not look at the speck, look at your log. We say we love Jesus but we follow our bishops we tells us to look at the speck and ignore our logs. So then why are surprised that enmity has not ended. What kind of a disciple are you who changes what your Lord says? Do you know where that comes from? Your heart. Both blacks and whites have hearts that are filled with vices. Technology and science has not changed that. Please note, I am not asking you to continue pointing figures (we are very good at that). I am asking you to examine your heart as I do mine before the Lord Jesus.